Feast of Laughter

An Appreciation of R. A. Lafferty

Centenary First Edition   November 7, 2014

Other writers are influences. Lafferty is a revelation.

Ktistec Press

Feast of Laughter
An Appreciation of R. A. Lafferty
Edition 1, November 7, 2014
Published by The Ktistec Press

Cover painting: Lissanne Lake
Cover layout: David Morrow

"The Six Fingers of Time" by R. A. Lafferty is currently in the public domain. The text used is from Project Gutenberg (http://www.gutenberg.org/ebooks/31663).

ISBN-13: 978-0692324103
ISBN-10: 0692324100

DEDICATION

This volume is the work of a very dedicated group of Lafferty fans. If an author's work can be judged not by the number of his books in print or the volume of his sales, but rather by the avidity of his fans, then R. A. Lafferty must be seen as the one of the most important writers in the history of the written word.

This volume is dedicated to all the Lafferty fans, librarians, and small-press publishers who strived for decades to keep his writing alive.

Most especially, it is dedicated to the memory of R. A. Lafferty —both the man and his writing—on this, his 100th birthday.

Happy Birthday, Ray!

TABLE OF CONTENTS

ACKNOWLEDGMENTS

This volume would not have been possible without the valiant effort of many dedicated (dare I say rabid?) fans. Acknowledgment is due to every person in the list of contributors.

Visit the R. A. Lafferty fan group on Facebook, "East of Lafferty" to see all these wonderful people in action, talking about Lafferty—his writing and his life—and perhaps planning the next edition: https://www.facebook.com/groups/eastoflaughter/

Look to the Feast of Laughter website for this and future issues of this humble 'zine: http://www.feastoflaughter.org

Feast of Laughter

THE ORIGIN OF THE FEAST
by Kevin Cheek

An introduction to Feast of Laughter, Edition 1

Much can be said for the Internet and social media. R. A. Lafferty's work is almost entirely out of print—except for *Okla Hannali*, available in a beautiful Print on Demand edition from the University of Oklahoma Press. However, an ever-growing handful of fans has connected over the internet, sharing tips on finding books, pontificating and propounding on his stories, occasionally arguing over his Catholicism, but—perhaps odd for an online gathering of rabid fans—supporting each other more often than criticising, and welcoming each new and different point of view. Such is the power of Lafferty's work. Was his writing destined to a slow slide into obscurity? Has the sharing of fandom over the Internet helped save Lafferty's writing from this fate? Perhaps not, but the fact that you are reading this zine is evidence that awareness of his work is growing, and in this particular instance, it could not have happened without the internet.

It started back sometime in the '90s. In the early days of what we know as the popular Internet (back when Netscape Navigator was the browser of choice and Google wasn't even a gleam in a grad student's eye), a German computer engineer going by the handle Nat! created the Lafferty Devotional Page. He posted one-sentence reviews and ratings of almost everything Lafferty ever wrote, including some unpublished stories. Bulletin board software allowed fans (still a small group online) to communicate and exchange ideas. Those few Lafferty fans who stumbled upon his site rejoiced in finding like-minded people and such a great resource. Fortunately for us all, the Lafferty Devotional Page is still up and its forums are alive with discussion.

Then writers, essayists, and reviewers started posting their comments, essays, and reviews of Lafferty's writing online. There was Don Webb's excellent analysis, "Effective Arcanum," Eric Walker's essay on "Science-Fiction and Fantasy Books by R. A. Lafferty," John J. Reilly's review of *The Flame is Green*. Add to that the small press publishers who posted the introductions from their by-then out-of-print volumes: "Sometimes They Took the Sky off at Night" by Brian Cholfin and "Despair and the Duck Lady" by Michael Swanwick. By this time the internet was—well, not exactly brimming with Lafferty-related content, but there was content out there for the devoted fans to find.

Recent years have seen the birth of blogging and social media. In the blogosphere, Daniel Petersen started "The Ants of God are Queer Fish" and Andrew Ferguson started "Continued on Next Rock" as an outlet for his scholarly work on Lafferty. More blogs soon followed, and it appears that things are reaching a critical mass.

In social media, David Cruces created a Lafferty fan group called "East of Laughter" after Lafferty's surreal (irreal? subreal?) novel about a quest for "real" reality. This group has become more populous and more vocal over the past year, attracting the rabid Lafferty fans — the deeply erudite Lafferty fans, binge-reading fans, and even occasional fans who like a story here and a story there, but like them strongly enough to join the conversation.

In discussion the other day, members of the group were discussing SF fanzines with Lafferty content. Someone piped up that we needed our own zine, and someone suggested almost off-hand the title "Feast of Laughter." But this really wasn't an off-hand remark. First, it mimics the name of the group. Second, it resonates with Dan Knight's Introduction to his magazine in Tribute to R.A. Lafferty, "The Boomer Flats Gazette," in which he compares appreciation of Lafferty's stories to sharing a feast:

> *T*he table was prepared and the bar was stocked for as big a bash as ever was seen. There was something for everyone. A magical feast. Take as much as you want. Stuff your pockets and fill your purse. It would make no difference. There would be just as much when you were done as when you started. This is fish and loaves stuff. (Are not all good stories fish and loaves stuff by their very definition?)

And third, most importantly, laughter is a strong part of Lafferty's storytelling. Can you read any of his stories without a deep belly-chuckle? Sometimes the more horrifying stories contain the strongest humor, and sometimes, like in "Hog Belly Honey", every sentence is such a joy to read, you laugh yourself nearly comatose before half finishing the story.

The fans hit the ground running and started assembling submissions. This has been a labor of love, extreme effort, and massive communication. Amazingly, not four weeks from that first mention on a Facebook fan group, this "Feast of Laughter" served for your consumption.

Bon appétit!

Kevin Cheek is a Lafferty fan and professional technical writer. He blogs infrequently at www.yetanotherlaffertyblog.com

TALKING ABOUT TALKING ABOUT LAFFERTY

by Kevin A. Cheek

To talk on Lafferty for one whole day
Would call for no great effort on my part
There really is an awful lot to say
And any phrase for me's a place to start

Expound on archetypes both old and new
And how for character they often stand
And how repeated phrases form a glue
To lead us through a story by the hand

A writer steeped in deep mythology
Theology Medieval, erudite
A Catholic writer of philosophy
Who went at last most faithful into night.

But wiser heads perhaps should have their say
Before I ramble on for one whole day.

LAFFERTOGRAPHY
by Rich Persaud

"Are you human or robot?" the computer prompted impolitely. "Type the characters shown in the image." A few offended responses later, it bestowed upon me permission to enter. I am human, until the next test.

"Are you worthy?" the Lafferty stories inquired nonchalantly. "Decode the sounds told." I stop. Which sounds? I hear the dry verdict of the Guardian of the Holy Grail in Indiana Jones and the Last Crusade. "He chose ... poorly." It can be risky to knock upon encoded doors to protected treasures. On which story should I knock? Is there a map of Lafferty treasures?

If we will get out of Lafferty only what we're equipped to bring in (Theodore Sturgeon), each reading is a singular event. The experience of reading a Lafferty story alters what readers will bring, the next time around. Treasure maps are transformed. As John Ellison notes in this volume, "We often can't go back into the first evocations and ambiance felt when reading a particular Lafferty story."

This volume's essays by Elaine Cochrane and Eric Walker can precede or follow a new reader's first Lafferty experience. Cochrane offers to new readers a guided tour of Lafferty waypoints and doors upon which to knock. Walker offers safety nets and decoder rings to treasure seekers who have chosen their point of entry, and who wish to deepen their first, unrepeatable Lafferty experience.

Eighteen years after Cochrane's 1996 observation of a "tiny trickle of Lafferty material still being published", Lafferty's works remain out of print, with the exception of Okla Hannali and collector editions that sell out quickly. However, the Cordwainer Smith website notes on their Lafferty Rediscovery Award page, "... now you can find many of them somewhere on the net."

One constant remains — the need for literary criticism of Lafferty's works. Layers of hidden treasure await repeat readers. Lafferty's writing attracts a diverse audience, whose search for critiques inexorably leads them to each other. In their quest to decode his timeless stories, Lafferty's readers are creating a unique body of work. In this volume, they joyously risk knocking. Their inspiration is his legacy.

"Are you worthy?" the Lafferty stories inquired nonchalantly.

Choose ... wisely.

Rich Persaud has worked in software & sales engineering, product & program management, business development and management consulting. He created http://RALafferty.org in October 2014, to help introduce new readers to Lafferty's works.

A FEW WORDS ABOUT R. A. LAFFERTY
by Eric Walker

Raphael Aloysius "Ray" Lafferty, the self-described "cranky old man from Tulsa, Oklahoma," is a genius: I state that flatly. He is one of the eminent English-language writers of, at the very least, the twentieth century—yet he remains little known, little read, and much misunderstood and under-appreciated. Indeed, much of his oeuvre exists only in very limited print runs of cheap paper chapbooks.

As the thoughtful will deduce, the problem is that Lafferty is not an easy writer. That problem is exacerbated by the fact that under superficial consideration he looks easy; were he as obviously complex as, for example, James Joyce (and, of course, were he not "just" an SF&F author), readers and critics would likely have made some effort to look beneath the hood to see what was what; but because his works can, by the careless, be taken for ordinary stuff, his complexities—of both language and meaning—end up dismissed as just nonsensically bad ordinary writing. As a thirsty drinker expecting the taste of a soda pop might well spit out in disgust a mouthful of vintage brut champagne, so might an SF reader expecting typical SF reject vintage Lafferty.

Even experienced readers of SF&F, accustomed to unusual and complicated tales and worlds, can find Lafferty puzzling or worse at first blush. So, before I attempt to set out some of Lafferty's excellences, let me say a bit about what one needs to know to even begin to grasp his work.

Lafferty is never "realistic." However ordinary his settings may seem when first we start one of his tales, we must remember that for a certainty they are surreal fantasies in the truest sense of those words. I think the most apt analogy for Lafferty's works is animated cartoons. Things in Lafferty tales happen at the breathless, breakneck pace—and with the madcap ad hoc paralogic —of a Bugs Bunny cartoon. We believe none of it because we are never for a second expected to believe any of it, any more than we are expected to "believe" what happens to Bugs and Elmer; we do not participate to behold "slices of life" but to behold madcap exaggerations and distortions of it. The single worst error a reader new to Lafferty can make is to think that a world Lafferty introduces in apparently ordinary science-fiction terms actually is (even by science-fiction standards) ordinary.

Well, look here:

> *T*he ichthyans or Queer Fish are the oddest species to be found in any of the worlds. They are pseudo-human, perhaps, but not android. The sign of the fish is not easily seen on them,

and they pass as human whenever they wish: a peculiarity of them is that they often do not wish to pass as human even when their lives depend on it. They have blood in their veins, but an additional serum as well. It is only when the organizational sickness is upon them (for these organizing and building proclivities they are sometimes known as the Queer Builders or the Ants of God), that they can really be told from humans. . . . Their threat to us is more real than apparent and we tend to minimize it. This we must not do. In our unstructured, destructed, destroyed society, they must be counted as the enemies to be exterminated. It's a double danger they offer to us: to fight them on their own grounds, or to neglect to fight them. They'd almost trick us into organizing to hunt down their organization.

You are forewarned that there must be some sort of twist here, but a casual reader, ignorant of Lafferty, skimming that in a bookstore, might take it for a particularly sloppy routine s.f. tale of aliens. Instead, we come to find, the "Queer Fish" (think "fish" bumper stickers) are the few Godly folk remaining in the modernist "unstructured, destructed, destroyed society" that Lafferty continually maintains we are rapidly becoming (or perhaps have already become). It's just Lafferty's way of speaking.

To know that all of Lafferty's works are surreal is necessary but not sufficient for understanding those works: we need to consider the ways in which that surrealism commonly manifests itself. The commonest way is a disdain for time, which is almost always highly telescoped down in Lafferty tales (as in animated cartoons) so as to keep the focus tightly on the wild action going on in the main ring:

"When are your friends going to arrive, Epikt?" Valery Mok asked that creative machine who was presently in his modified alligator mobile extension. "Not that I greatly look forward to their arrival, but there's a lot of spooky literature arriving here in care of them. That little magazine Okkult, ugh!"

"They will arrive within minutes or seconds," Epikt conveyed in a cavernous sort of voice. "That little magazine Okkult, ugh! contains an article of my own, 'The Gravity of Hollow Spheres', made up entirely of anomalies. I'm proud of it."

"Epikt, do you know what happened to the water in Lake Yahola Reservoir?" Gregory Smirnov the Director of the Institute for Impure Science asked sharply. "The early morning report has it that all the water disappeared with a great sucking sound within two minutes. That was only half an hour ago."

"All the water in the reservoir went down a big hole in the ground," Epikt uttered. "I hate it when things go wrong like that. They were about five miles off."

"Epikt, do you know what's making all the big holes in Donner's Pasture?" Aloysius Shiplap asked. "Half a dozen houses have already slipped into them, and there's consternation among the people of the neighborhood."

"*T*hey're coming closer," Epikt said. "They'll be here pretty quick now. Tell the people that no harm was intended, that they can have their houses back again if they want to go down in the holes and get them. My friends are trying to navigate by themselves, and a trip like this is a first."

We don't *believe* any of that is happening or could happen or might happen in any version of the world we know, but who cares? We watch for much the same reasons we watch the obviously unreal, surreal antics of Bugs and Elmer (and Porky and Daffy and Sylvester)—because those antics are stupendously amusing.

Lafferty has many excellences. To touch on one in passing, one you have already seen a bit of, there's his genius with character names: the names he gives out in his tales make it clear that we are in strange territory. Here's a most abbreviated roll call, as if what you have already read weren't enough!: Anthony Longarm; Caspar O'Malley; Andrew Giro; Basil Cubic; Theophile Marzials; Fairbridge O'Boyle; Benny B-Flat; Dirk Stroeve; Ester Jack; Bruno Starlight; Adrian Mansion; Shalimar McGuire; Arsine Braveheart; Alfred Freck; Catherine Klutz; Jimpson Ginseng; Johnny Greeneyes; Darius Parsee; Jack Bang; Dr. Velikov Vonk; Flip O'Grady (a chimpanzee); George Meropen; Griggles Swing; Abel Riordan; Belinda Greenglow; Victor Hornspoon; Honest Schzhoultsko; Henry Sounder; Diamant Harp; Joe Greatglobe; Rambo Touchstone; Karl Effigy; Clement Stringtown; Crowley Headcooper; Hildebrand Oakley; Robert Straitroad; Redman Newbreeze; Culpepper Geier; George Artless; Lemuel Windfall; Ronald Kolibri; Bonta Chrysalis; Michael Goodgrind; Ignace Wolff; Joseph Waterwitch; Vincent Rue; Adrian Durchbruch; and, as the King reputedly said, et cetera, et cetera, et cetera.

The lot sound like names from Jackie Gleason's old "Joe the Bartender" stories—remember Gaylord Farquhart? Many of those delightfully named persons recur throughout Lafferty's tales, sometimes as major players and sometimes as "cameos"; among the "regulars"—and if that sounds like a neighborhood bar, perhaps that is not coincidental—are the members of the Institute for Impure Science, most of whom you have now already met; Austro, a twelve-year-old "general-purpose genius of the species australopithecus" and co-author of the Rocky McCrocky comic strip; the eminent scientist Willy McGilly; Roy Mega; Audifax O'Hanlon; Mary Mondo (a ghost); Diogenes Pontifex; et, as one says, alia. There will be a quiz in the morning; as a study key, consider the preponderant nature of the surnames. There are some further notes below at the heading Lafferty's Universes.

A telescoping of time is but one of Lafferty's characteristic surrealities. Another is simple, but hard to *describe* simply. It is the trick of having all the characters in a tale understand each other perfectly, without question, despite the zany and impossible nature of most everything each is saying and doing, just as in—yet again —a Bugs Bunny cartoon. They, like Bugs, live in their peculiar world, not ours, however much it may *look* like our world. Lafferty is by no means the only writer ever to use this mannerism: Charles Finney uses it in several tales; Flann O'Brien used it; others have too. (Do we see a pattern here? Do you recall your study key?)

But so far I may be giving you the impression that Lafferty is some sort of American Tom Holt or Terry Pratchett, a master comedian. Well, Lafferty, like those two fine writers, is indeed at times largely a comic (none of them are ever "entirely" comic— there's always a bite in that comedy); but were that the limit of Lafferty, he'd not be on my five-star list. No, much of the time— *most* of the time—Lafferty is a very great deal more than "merely" funny. While his house brand of manic humor permeates all of his work, the bulk of that work is far more complex and freighted than, for example, the cavortings of Austro and Roy Mega.

That brings us to the next key a reader needs to unlock Lafferty's code: Lafferty is a devout, conservative Roman Catholic, and his strongly held beliefs pervade and indeed power all his major works. Moreover, while Lafferty's encyclopedic knowledge of Catholic lore (and lore in general, for that matter) is spread throughout his tales, those tales invariably focus on what Lafferty clearly sees as *the* central malady of our time: the collapse of values—a problem that goes beyond any one particular religion or even philosophy, and so gives a powerful vitality and universality to Lafferty's curiously coded visions.

Mind, Lafferty does not spin grim morality plays: he tells stories, very zany stories with a lot of fun juice in them. A quotation from Navarth the mad poet (creation of Lafferty's contemporary Jack Vance) is strikingly apposite to Lafferty and his works:

> *I* sought to express truth in all its vehemence. This is a danger. A meaning must be uttered idly, without emphasis. The listener is under no compulsion to react; his customary defenses are not in place, the meaning enters his mind.

To repeat: while Lafferty's tellings occasionally include ideas specific to Roman Catholic doctrine (as in *Tales of Midnight*, for example), those tales nonetheless have essentially universal applicability, in that Lafferty is much more concerned with matters so fundamental that exactly what values one may have are far less important than that one have values. The catastrophe of modern times (in his essays, Lafferty makes plain his belief that this disease exploded into virulence in the mid to late twentieth century, a thought with which many would concur) is the degrading of the very concept of values, of the very idea of any thing or things being worth more than any other thing or things, being worth anything at all. He does not "deplore" the **"Whatever. . ."** era: he despises it with a hatred fathoms deep.

(In the interests of full disclosure, I should say that while my metaphysics and Lafferty's are pretty far apart, his and my ethics are very close. I agree with him that this bleaching to gray of everything important—the world-view that I sum up in the phrase No Values—is the crucial problem of our time.)

Lafferty is passionate and is crying out in a poet's tongue, but we can see on all sides of us what he means: just pick up any daily newspaper. However insane you think something, if it isn't in today's news, it'll be in tomorrow's. It is the outlook so aptly expressed near the beginning of the century by Aleister Crowley, the self-styled "Great Beast": ***Do what thou wilt shall be the whole of the Law***. We see it everywhere: in "grammar manuals" that tell us that "good English" is whatever the most people say; in movies and television series where vicious gangsters are the "heroes"; in the continual "dumbing-down" of schooling; and on and on—pick up that newspaper and read. Lafferty is—as am I— sick of that horrid flattening-out process, that steam-rollering of all human values in the name of "the higher value."

Let us look again at that passage about the "Queer Fish." It comes from *And Walk Now Gently Through the Fire*, a work from Lafferty's earlier days—what we might call his *Portrait of the Artist* phase—when he was (like Joyce in that period) relatively clear, at least compared to what came later. The world of that tale (as always, painted by Lafferty with wild surrealism) is the post-modern "unstructured, destructed, destroyed society" that its correspondingly "unstructured, destructed, destroyed" members think is wonderful, having lost the ability to see that they cannot see, realize that they cannot realize, understand that they cannot understand. Everything Lafferty says in that tale is heavily freighted with overtones that are invisible if one does not have the key, plain—almost obvious—if one does.

> *H*ow is a person or a world unmade or unformed? First, by being deformed. And following the deforming is the collapsing. The tenuous balance is broken. Insanity is induced easily under the name of the higher sanity. Then the little candle that is in each head is blown out on the pretext that the great cosmic light can better be seen without it."

The process is not some great uprising of evil, easy to see, to rally against: it is insidious, it creeps, it overtakes the unwary:

> *T*he persons and the worlds were never highly stable. A cross-member is removed here on the pretext of added freedom. Foundation blocks are taken away on the pretext of change. Supporting studs are pulled down on the pretext of new experience. And none of the entities had ever been supported more strongly than was necessary. What happens then? A man collapses, a town, a city, a nation, a world. And it is hardly noticed.

That, to Lafferty, is how evil triumphs: it erases, it reduces, it boils down; it destroys intellect, individuality; it depersonalizes. The monsters it creates do not slaver and torture and rend flesh: they trade stock options and take three weeks in Bermuda and swap wives and starve the poor and blow up cities with jaunty gaiety, literal mindlessness. They have the desires, and the morals, and the minds, of small children. They pull the wings off flies and the heads off people because it is so amusing. The one crime, the one sin, left available, is to fail to pursue gaiety with sufficient force—to assert values or individual personality, individual thoughts; and if you do that, gray faceless men come and take you away, and no one cares because you were just an old wet blanket anyway. Recall the phrase *Kraft durch Freude;* recall other cautionary tales, *Brave New World, That Hideous Strength* (C. S. Lewis).

But there now, I have been putting the cart before the horse: I have gotten from Lafferty prerequisites into the ways in which Lafferty—himself a mad poet if ever there was one—stimulates the reader's mental processes. Let us backtrack to the four basic elements of pleasing readers.

Lafferty's language you have seen a bit of. His is not the pastel elegance of a Lord Dunsany, not the mordant irony of a Jack Vance; his is the smooth, flowing Blarney of a poet drunk on (at the least) words. Several observers have likened his style to that of traditional folk "tall tales," and there is a clear resemblance.

With some writers, and Lafferty is one, small samples do not work well, for much of such writers' effect is by the sustaining of a tone: a snapshot of someone standing on a wire is necessarily less astounding than seeing that person walking that long tightwire in perfect balance.

Having done as much as anything less than reading Lafferty at one or more books' length can do to display his wondrous and delightful language (or so I hope), I turn to the other three elements of pleasing readers: plot, settings, and characterization. And here are difficulties.

Lafferty's plots, his settings, his characterizations are as bizarrely jumbled as his language. The tale you are reading is never the tale he is telling. (The more I reflect on Lafferty, the more significant that statement seems.) Lafferty tells tales of the timeless things, the things of enduring—of *eternal*—value, the ways of the worlds visible and invisible, the human psyche and (unfashionable thought in our increasingly "unstructured, destructed, destroyed" society) the human soul. But he does not tell his real tales in the way a C. S. Lewis (for example) would, straightforwardly and covered only with a fictive gauze so sheer as to plainly have been selected so as to not chance the weakest eye not penetrating it (much less in the flashing-neon-illuminated style of so many who have not made these lists at all); Lafferty presents his real tales as what we may perhaps consider parables— sometimes as obvious as most of the things we are used to encountering under that rubric and sometimes, to put it mildly, arcane—almost opaque.

In a Lafferty tale—a Lafferty hyperparable—the plot, the settings, the characters are a swirling snowstorm of symbology, sometimes naively plain and sometimes hauled up from deep in the Jungian racial memory or the collective unconscious (Lafferty disdains such notions but is nevertheless fluent in both their formal terminology and their actual content). To shift metaphor, Lafferty fires these symbols at us like a manic machine-gunner; they interweave, they burn the air; they hit their targets, they miss wildly; but the gunner keeps his finger locked to the trigger. It is hard to read a sentence of Lafferty, impossible to read a paragraph, without being hit by one or more symbolic names or acts, sometimes large, sometimes small.

Understand that while Lafferty's works are woven almost wholly of symbol-thread, they are not allegories. In allegory, the tale you *are* reading is comprehensible, a simplified playing out of the tale the author wants to tell. Lafferty is telling the tales he wants to tell in a waving of symbols akin to the frantic waving of arms of a mute pregnant with vital news. Lafferty waves, he dances, he plays intellectual charades with us; but he does not deal in allegory.

To close the circle: Lafferty's core message is invariable—the good must resist the mindbreakers, must not yield to the pleasures of mindless pleasure, must do what is often hard and painful.

(Lafferty is often quite casually quite gruesome in describing what the wicked do to the good. Folk are, in almost jolly descriptions, disemboweled, throat-slit, pulled to pieces, burned to ash, or sent to any number of other curious but repellent fates. Sometimes they are killed, but more often they are translated to some peculiar status in the tale, a ghostly or, on occasion, even solid (if decidedly unusual) presence, or entombed awaiting some future event, which may come within the tale or only be implied.)

So that's R. A. Lafferty: profound parables of things eternal presented as manic animated cartoons written down in the language of a mad poet. If you cannot readily imagine such a thing, I have two comments: one, I'd be a little worried if you could; and two, go read a few Lafferty books. You will be changed, and possibly improved, by the experience.

Lafferty's Universes

As I remarked somewhere above, Lafferty commonly shoves many curious names at us in his tales, often as a long list not needful to the tale itself ("Some of the persons who made up that golden age were . . . .") and so plainly included for humor or other value; moreover, many of those names surface repeatedly. The attentive and patient reader going through the entire corpus of Lafferty's works could use those repeating names to thread together otherwise unrelated tales into a larger montage or universe. I have never undertaken the task (it's the "patient" quality I lack), but I wouldn't be surprised if most or even all of his novels, as well as a large fraction of his short stories, could be so tied together.

All that said, Lafferty's works seem to revolve around three chief foci. The first of those foci is The Institute For Impure Science, and orbiting it are the novel *Arrive at Easterwine* and a large number of short stories, notably those in *Through Elegant Eyes: Stories of Austro and the Men Who Know Everything* but going back to some of Lafferty's earliest work. In these tales we encounter—among many—Gregory Smirnov, Valery Mok, Charles Cogsworth, Aloysius Shiplap, and of course Epikt, the Ktistec machine, chief figure of *Arrive at Easterwine*, and whom you have seen in action in some of the quotations above; this focus also centers the Austro stories, which you have also tasted above.

Another node of Lafferty's tales is what I suppose we might call the "future outer space" focus. This includes reference to the worlds of Astrobe and Klepsis and many more, and orbiting it are such novels as *Past Master, Space Chantey, The Annals of Klepsis*, and possibly others, plus many, many of his short stories.

The third focus is the *Argo* mythos, centered on the idea of the ship *Argo*—yes, the one Jason sailed—as a mystic and eternal craft (symbolic, to Lafferty, of the Catholic Church) sailing in and out of space, time, and history. Most of the books orbiting this focus are so labelled in the book list farther below, but very possibly others of Lafferty's tales also feel its gravitational pull.

As I said, the fanatic, with patience, could probably link all of Lafferty's works. There is, for instance, in one of the *Argo* books, the bare mention—in one of those laundry lists of names—of one

Aloysius Shiplap, which could justify tying the Institute tales to the world of the *Argo* tales; and there are doubtless other such fragile connects. (For example, Enniscorthy Sweeney's name also appears.)

But none of that is really important. I mention the foci only because the reader new to Lafferty needs as many assists as possible, just as one first learning trapeze work needs safety lines and nets till enough skill is acquired to sail fearlessly through the air with trust that the next trapeze bar will be where its needed when it's needed—and so it is with reading Lafferty. Knowing a little about the foci of his work just helps keep everything a little less disorganized.

There is little or no middle ground on Lafferty: one either doesn't at all like his work, or one thinks it genius. As many commentators have observed over the years, Lafferty is the proverbial "caviar to the masses", and very few of his works ever sold well to the general public. As often happens to talented writers with a taste for the speculative, he fell between two bar stools: too literary for the genre fans, and too genre-"tainted" for the *soi-disant* literati.

Lafferty, like other prolific yet under-appreciated authors, is hard to sort into a coherent bibliography. Anything you find by him—anything—read and enjoy. The world is not always ready for genius: much of Lafferty's work has yet to see print for the first time, while so much more is now so rare as to be wildly expensive when available at all.

There has never yet been a complete and correct edition of the keystone novel *The Devil Is Dead*. Two different parts—an "Interglossia" and a brief final chapter—have been omitted from all editions to date. (The Interglossia appeared in *How Many Miles to Babylon?,* while the final chapter appeared in *Episodes of the Argo.*)

I have often wished for something closely analogous to the Vance Integral Edition project to be undertaken for Lafferty's work, though most regrettably the author himself is no longer available for consultation. But a well-edited uniform set would be a wonder and a marvel. (And a companion volume of essays a choice extension.)

I, and I'm sure many others, look forward to Lafferty's republication with unabated eagerness.

Eric Walker (http://owlcroft.com) has worked in aerospace, radio broadcasting, property management, taxicab driving, the legal industry and statistical baseball analysis. As consultant to the sympathetic and intelligent front office of the Oakland Athletics, he had an enduring effect on analytic principles and philosophy that lead to the A's immense success documented in Moneyball.

IF YOU DO NOT LOVE WORDS:
THE PLEASURE OF READING LAFFERTY
by Elaine Cochrane

(Author's note: The following was written for presentation to
the Nova Mob (Melbourne's SF discussion group), 2 October
1996, and was not intended for publication. I don't even get around
to listing my favourite Lafferty stories.)

Raphael Aloysius Lafferty was born in Iowa in 1914, and
moved to Oklahoma at the age of four. Apart from four and a half
years' army service he lived there ever since. He worked as an
electrical engineer. In his biography at the start of *Past Master*
(Ace, 1968), he writes "I was a heavy drinker till about eight years
ago at which time I cut down on it, beginning my writing attempts
at the same time to fill up a certain void."

Most of his some 150 short stories and 20-odd novels (including several non-SF) were published in the 1960s and 1970s; the Hugo-winning short story "Eurema's Dam" appeared in 1972, and the most recent short story I've tracked down was published in 1995. Most references I've come across say he stopped writing in the 1980s because of ill health, which implies that the trickle of short stories appearing since then is mainly desk-drawer stuff. Perhaps; but many of the early short stories appeared in the *Orbit* collections and *Galaxy*, *If* and *F&SF*; the anthology *Nine Hundred Grandmothers* was published by Ace and *Strange Doings* and *Does Anyone Else Have Something Further to Add?* by Scribners, and the novels were published by Avon, Ace, Scribners and Berkley. The anthologies and novels since then have been small press publications, and many of the short stories are still to be collected into anthologies, suggesting that a declining output has coincided with a declining market.

Lafferty says of his work, quoted in *Twentieth-Century Science-Fiction Writers* (3rd ed., St James Press 1991), "My novels, which I wrote myself at great labor, have received more attention than my short stories, which wrote themselves. Nevertheless, the short stories are greatly superior to the novels."

He is unclassifiable as to genre. His settings include other planets, and his stories sometimes feature spaceships and often the interactions between non-human species, but as Sandra Miesel says in *Twentieth-Century Science-Fiction Writers*, "There is not a bit of science in Lafferty's SF". He has technology coexisting with doubles and fetches and ghosts, but with the matter-of-fact flavour of magic realism and myth rather than the fantastic flavour of sword and sorcery. And he is often very funny. Miesel describes him as "science fiction's most prodigious teller of tall tales".

One thing that makes Lafferty special is his style. He loves language. In *Arrive at Easterwine* (Scribners, 1971) he has

Epiktistes, the computer who is the putative author of the book, introduce the work:

> **O**h, come along, reader of the High Journal; if you do not love words, how will you love the communication? How will you forgive me my tropes, communicate the love?

and the entire novel is a joyful celebration of language.

He delights in the sounds of words. In "Ginny Wrapped in the Sun" (1967, in *Nine Hundred Grandmothers*, Ace, 1970):

> "***I**m* going to read my paper tonight, Dismas," Dr Minden said, "and they'll hoot me out of the hall. [...] Hauser honks like a gander! That clattering laugh of Goldbeater! Snodden sniggers so loud that it echoes! Cooper's boom is like barrels rolling downstairs, and your own — it'll shrivel me, Dismas."

and in jokes: "It is no ignorant man who tells you this. I have read the booklets in your orderly tents: Physics without Mathematics, Cosmology without Chaos, Psychology without Brains" ("The Cliffs That Laughed", 1968, in *Strange Doings*, Scribners, 1972).

Rhyme is used frequently, just for the fun of it and as a structural device (e.g. the chapter openings in *Space Chantey*, all dreadful doggerel and deliberately painful rhymes), but more importantly as a story element. For example, the Pucas, the visiting aliens in *Reefs of Earth* (Berkley, 1968), use "Bagarthach verses" to curse hostile humans: "Old Crocker man, be belled and banged!/You hound-dog hunk, we'll have you hounded!/On else than gallows be you hanged! In else than water be you drownded!" and in the delightful "The Transcendent Tigers" (1964, in *Strange Doings*), the children shout rhymes as they jab a needle into a map:

> "*P*eas and Beans—/New Orleans!" She jabbed the needle into New Orleans on the map, and the great shaft a hundred thousand miles long came down into the middle of the Crescent City. [then, several cities later]
>
> "I know one," said Eustace, and he clapped the red cap on his own head:
>
> "Eggs and Batter —
>
> Cincinnater."
>
> He rhymed and jabbed, manfully but badly.
>
> "That didn't rhyme very good," said Carnadine. "I bet you botched it."
>
> He did. It wasn't a clean-cut holocaust at all. It was a clumsy, bloody, grinding job — not what you'd like.

The delight in language extends to mythological and literary puns and allusions. I've probably missed most of them; here are a few I've spotted.

The demon-like aliens in *The Reefs of Earth* are called Pucas; "pwca" is the Welsh version of Puck, and I suspect that the Irish name is much the same: in Flann O'Brien's *At Swim Two Birds* the demon is called "the Pooka". (Although in *The Devil is Dead* we are told that the Irish for Devil is Ifreann.)

In *Not to Mention Camels* (Bobbs-Merrill, 1976), a character aspires to archetype status; and among the already existing archetypes listed there is Gyne Peri-bebleene-ton- Helion (Woman-Wrapped-in-the-Sun) (p. 155) — compare the short-story title "Ginny Wrapped in the Sun".

The author of "a series of nineteen interlocked equations of cosmic shapeliness and simplicity", of which "it was almost as though nothing else could ever be added on any subject whatsoever" is one Professor Aloys Foucault-Oeg. ("Aloys", *Strange Doings*.)

In "Thus We Frustrate Charlemagne" (1967, in *Nine Hundred Grandmothers*) members of the Institute of Impure Science have built a high-tech device they call an Avatar in order to tamper with the past:

> "*I* hope the Avatar isn't expensive," Willy McGilly said. "When I was a boy we got by with a dart whittled out of slippery elm wood."
>
> "This is no place for humor," Glasser protested. "Who did you, as a boy, ever kill in time, Willy?"
>
> "Lots of them. King Wu of the Manchu, Pope Adrian VII, President Hardy of our own country, King Marcel of Auvergne, the philosopher Gabriel Toeplitz. It's a good thing we got them. They were a bad lot."

"But I never heard of any of them, Willy," Glasser insisted.

"Of course not. We killed them when they were kids."

Glasser may not have heard of any of them, but Hadrian VII is the biography of a fictitious pope written by Baron Corvo, the equally fictitious persona of the writer Frederick Rolfe. I wouldn't mind betting that the others have similar references that I haven't identified.

The short stories are very varied. They tend to be conventionally structured developments of an idea, often enlivened and sometimes burdened by expository lumps.

Often the expository lump is given in the form of a quotation from some reference, such as "The Back Door of History" by Arpad Arutinov, or the writings of Diogenes Pontifex or Audifax O'Hanlon, two worthies excluded from the Institute of Impure Science by the minimum decency rule.

The novels also tend to be idea-driven rather than plot-driven, and this is not always enough to tie them together. In the first edition of *The Encyclopedia of Science Fiction* (ed. Nicholls, Granada, 1979), John Clute describes the novels *The Devil is Dead* and *Arrive at Easterwine* as tangled; in the new edition (ed. Clute and Nicholls, Orbit, 1993) he says of *Arrive at Easterwine* that "it begins to evince a tangledness that comes, at times, close to incoherence". Miesel says of the same novels that Lafferty "mistakes the accumulation of vignettes for the construction of a novel."

I've enjoyed *Arrive at Easterwine* both times I've read it, as

I've been carried along by the exuberance of the writing. Of the others I've read, *Past Master* comes closest to a conventional plot, although I was disappointed when I first read it some 15 years ago because I was looking for the same mad inventiveness that characterises the short stories. On re-reading it a couple of weeks ago I did find wonderful flashes of pure Lafferty humour, but like most of the novels it is essentially serious in intent and dark in mood. *Space Chantey* (Ace, 1968), which purports to be a retelling of the *Odyssey*, and *Annals of Klepsis* (Ace, 1983) are exceptions to this, and they do fit the description "a series of vignettes". There is the wonderful Lafferty humour in them, but not much else. At the other extreme, *Not to Mention Camels* (1976) and *Where Have You Been, Sandaliotis* (one of the two novels published in *Apocalypses*, Pinnacle, 1977), are typically quirky but are short on redeeming humour. *Not to Mention Camels* is almost embarrassingly gruesome.

Miesel says "So closely do Lafferty's novels resemble each other, they might as well be alternate drafts of the same story." A recurrent theme, particularly in the novels, is the battle between Good and Evil, but Lafferty has his own ideas of what these words mean. In "Horns on their Heads" (Pendragon Press, 1976, collected in *Iron Tears*, Edgewood Press, 1992), he writes:

> The "odor of sanctity" is not all lilacs and roses, nor is sanctity (the sacred, the sacer) a thing that stays within straited limits. It is too stark and rank for those limits. It pertains to holiness and sacredness; but also to awfulness; and further, to cursedness, to wickedness, execrability; to devotion; and again, to seizure and epilepsy.
>
> Now the "odor of sanctity", the smell of the

thing (stay with us; strong smells and stenches
are the vitality itself), is compounded of the
deepest and most eroding of sweating, the
sweating of blood and blood-serum; of nervous
and sweating muck of adrenal rivers; of the
excited fever of bodies and the quaking
deliriums of minds; of the sharp sanity of
igneous; and the bruised rankness of desert
bush. Oh, it is a strong and lively stench. It's the
smell of adoration, of passion seized in rigid
aestivation.

Clute refers to Lafferty's conservative Catholicism. I don't
know enough about Catholicism to pick up any references, but
Lafferty is strenuously life-affirming. Those fighting on the side of
"good" are fallible and sinners, and the battles are bloody and often
joyful; Lafferty rejects sterility and austerity and compromise and
"moderation in all things." Equally he rejects the attempts to
popularise and modernise the Church.

In *Past Master*, Sir Thomas More, being shown around the
planet Astrobe, asks Paul, his guide, to find him a church because
he wants to hear Mass:

Well, the replica mass ran its short course to
the jerking and bawling of the ancient ritual
guitar. At sermon time was given a straight
news-broadcast, so that one should not be out
of contact with the world for the entire fifteen
minutes.

At the Consecration, a sign lit up:

"Brought to you Courtesy of Grailo Grape-Ape,

31

the Finest of the Bogus Wines."

The bread was ancient-style hot-dog rolls. The puppets or mechanisms danced up orgasmically and used the old vein-needle before taking the rolls.

"How do you stop the dirty little thing?" Thomas asked.

"Push the *Stop* button," Paul said. "Here, I'll do it." And he stopped it. (p. 68)

Unusually for Lafferty, in *Past Master* the evil itself is given a name and a voice: it is Ouden, which means nothingness:

"*O*ld nothingness who sucks out the flames, I have known flames to be lighted again," said the Paul-Thomas.

"It will not kindle," said the Ouden. "I eat you up. I devour your substance. There was only one kindling. I was overwhelmed only once. But I gain on it. I have put it out almost everywhere. It will be put out forever here." [...]

"Never will I leave. Not ever in your life will you sit down that I do not sit down with you. And finally it will happen that only one of us is left to get up, and that will be myself. I suck you dry."

"I have one juice left that you do not know," said the Paul-Thomas.

"You have it less than you believe." (pp. 44–6)

Usually, however, Lafferty's evil is not some disembodied essence, but is manifest through the actions of people who have chosen to commit evil. Their acts are typically cruel, brutal and degraded, and recounted in gory detail. They are also often unconvincing. More convincing is Lafferty's depiction of the desire of those who have chosen evil to destroy the good:

Always the Lords could find a gnat's-weight of evidence against any man, and always that gnat's-weight would be enough to declare ruination.

Were they Lords of the Gnats for nothing? Many of these young Lords Spiritual had already scattered to hunt down and hamstring this great strong man.

For a people, even a good people, do not pass gnats easily, once they have gotten inside them. They will huff and puff and strain and turn purple, all over one adolescent gnat. And the gnat must be dissected, minutely dissected before it can be passed. It would never go out all in one piece. This selective passing is an oddity about even good people. They can pass out easily many very large objects, not to mention camels. (*Not to Mention Camels*, pp. 74-5)

A couple of short stories (such as "Or Little Ducks Each Day", in *Iron Tears*) feature patches or territories that belong to neither

God nor the Devil, and in many ways this sums up Lafferty's universe. Typically neither good nor evil triumphs; instead a sort of balance is restored with heavy casualties on both sides.

Lafferty's characters also have recurring types and themes. Children as the agents of gleeful chaos feature in a number of short stories. For example, seven-year-old Carnadine Thompson in "The Transcendent Tigers" is given her powers because "on that whole world I found only one person with perfect assurance — one impervious to doubt of any kind and totally impervious to self-doubt." In "All the People" (*Nine Hundred Grandmothers*), we read "Anthony had always had a healthy hatred for children and dogs, those twin harassers of the unfortunate and the maladjusted." In "Through Other Eyes" (*Nine Hundred Grandmothers*) "He learned ... the untarnished evil of small children, the diabolic possession of adolescents." In "Primary Education of the Camiroi", "small children are not yet entirely human". *Arrive at Easterwine* has: "Now then, tell me whether you have ever known an innocent child? Innocent, innocens, not-nocens, not noxious, not harming or threatening, not weaponed. Older persons may sometimes fall into a state of innocence (after they have lost their teeth and their claws), but children are never innocent if they are real. These four were real and not at all innocent." (p. 188)

His stories often feature outsiders — Gypsies, Native Americans, drunken Irish — who see the world in non-standard ways. There are often not-quite-humans living on the edges of or hidden within normal society.

"*T*here used to be a bunch of them on the edge of my home town," Willy McGilly said. "Come to think of it, there used to be a bunch of them on the edge of every hometown. Now they're more likely to be found right in the middle of every town. They're the scrubs, you know, for the bottoming of the breed." ("Boomer Flats", *Does Anyone Else Have Something Further to Add*, Scribners, 1974)

There are other remnants of older races, such as the predatory six-fingered pre-Babylonians in "The Six Fingers of Time" (*Nine Hundred Grandmothers*). I like the variant in "Adam Had Three Brothers" (*Does Anyone Else Have Something Further to Add?*):

Adam had three brothers: Etienne, Yancy, and Rreq. Etienne and Yancy were bachelors. Rreq had a small family and all his issue have had small families; until now there are about two hundred of them in all, the most who have ever been in the world at one time. They have never intermarried with the children of Adam except once. And not being of the same recension they are not under the same curse to work for a living.

So they do not.

Instead they batten on the children of Adam by clever devices that are known in police court as swindles.

Neanderthals recur many times, again sometimes but not always benign. For two benign examples, in *Not to Mention Camels* (pp. 4–5) Doctor Wilcove Funk is described in terms similar to those used to describe Dr Velikof Vonk in "Boomer Flats". Given the way Lafferty plays with names and swaps characters from story to story, the similarity of names and descriptions would be deliberate, although I can't guess to what purpose.

In *The Devil is Dead* (Avon, 1971), there is a battle taking place within the ranks of these pre-humans:

> "*T*he thing is biologically and genetically impossible. Was Mendel wrong? Were Morgan and Galton and Painter? Was even the great Asimov wrong? How is it possible to throw an angry primordial after a thousand generations? How is it possible to do it again and again?
>
> ... "Le Marin, you read about aliens from the stars who invade," Finnegan said. "Did you not know that there are nearer monsters and aliens?"
>
> "I know it, Monster, and you know it," said Le Marin, "but we do not want everyone to know it." (pp. 163–4)

As well as these there are the doubles and fetches, of planets as well as people, there is the taking over of minds and bodies, there are parallel universes, and playing around with the philosophic problems of perception, reality and illusion. Often simultaneously.

Does the tiny trickle of Lafferty material still being published reflect his output, or is it desk-drawer material, or is he simply unpublishable these days?

I suspect the answer is yes to all three questions. Lafferty's strength is the short story. The magazines that published much of his early work no longer exist, and the broad-based original fiction anthologies are largely replaced by invitation-only themed anthologies. And although it is possible to trace common threads and themes through much of Lafferty's work, he is difficult to categorise, and I cannot see him writing commissioned pieces for collections such as *Off Limits: Tales of Alien Sex* or *Lovecraft's Legacy*, and only just in *Fires of the Past: Thirteen Contemporary Fantasies about Hometowns*.

Elaine Cochrane (http://www.gillespiecochrane.com.au/) lives in suburban Melbourne, surrounded by books and cats. She works as a freelance editor of mainly science and medical books, and discovered the pleasure of reading Lafferty in 1970, when Ace published the anthology Nine Hundred Grandmothers.

AN INTERVIEW WITH JOHN PELAN
by John Owen

"*R*A. Lafferty is the greatest Axolotl Press author to never be published by Axolotl Press" - John Pelan

John Pelan is an author, editor, and small-press publisher, founder of Axolotl Press, Darkside Press, Silver Salamander Press, and co-founder of Midnight House. He has been working with Centipede Press to create their magnificent complete series of Lafferty stories. Their first volume, *The Man Who Made Models* came out in December, 2013. The second volume, *The Man with the Aura*, will be coming soon.

JRO: From April through June of this year, John Pelan graciously agreed to an interview over email. Multiple questions were collected from the fans at East of Lafferty and sent to John. His first response answered a number of questions specific to the scope and size of the Centipede project and his role in the project. After this initial response, John responded to the rest of the questions individually.

PELAN: Anyway, let's get a couple of fairly general queries out of the way right now. Is 12 books set in stone? No, of course not. That's a reasonable estimate made by a guy who didn't have all the material in hand when making the projection. Now let's kill two birds with one big ol' rock... At this point I do not know if we will be permitted to include a volume (or two) of unpublished material. Obviously, I would like to and equally obviously it makes sense for the owners of the Literary Estate to piggy-back on what Jerad and I are doing rather than attempting to reinvent the wheel. However, at this point we do not have the unpublished material under contract, though I am hopeful that we can come to terms.

Next, how does "the horror guy" come to be editing Lafferty (or for that matter, heading up the SF division of Centipede Press)? Well, to be succinct, I have always been a reader of imaginative literature, whether SF, fantasy, horror, rationalized supernatural, what have you. If it can be considered of the genre, I'll likely read it. For that matter, if it's of the mystery or modern lit genres, I'll likely as not to give it a whirl. I'm a real appreciator of the pre-WWII days when books weren't shoved into various market segments, but rather shelved under "fiction" or if the bookseller was really an organizer you might get "thrillers".

Anyway, you asked if there was any sort of plan behind my selections. Certainly, though it may not be readily apparent. What may seem desperately random isn't really random at all. These books are designed for two very distinct audiences (a.) the Lafferty fan who knows full well what they're getting into, and (b.) the reader who may be only vaguely familiar with the name and is impressed enough by the sheer volume of volumes (did I really just say that?), to want to check out a book in the series to see what all the fuss is about. So, with these two very different and equally important groups to consider, I've tried to duplicate how I originally read Lafferty!

Each book is like a publisher's party at a Worldcon: you'll find the familiar rubbing shoulders with the obscure, stories from the Elwood anthologies next to tales published in micro editions by Chris Drumm. The dark side by side with the humorous, the tales that at least use the tropes of SF beside those that are for lack of any other term, "modern folktales". The idea is that a person from either of those two main groups can pick up any volume, open to any story and discover R.A. Lafferty. I have deliberately eschewed the idea of presenting the works in other sort of order as I really don't care for collections that are ordered chronologically. There's just too much that can go wrong, the writer may go through a dry spell of mediocrity or perhaps a period where all the editors seem to be buying stories with a particular theme... In any event, if there are flaws (and every writer has them), there's no better way to reveal them than in a chronological collection.

I can't really duplicate the sensation of pawing through the SF magazines on the bottom two shelves at a dusty and very old bookstore, but I can *try* to get close. As to how well I did, I'll leave it to the reviewers to tell me.

JRO: How would you describe your relationship with Lafferty's fiction? Is he someone who you re-read often before this project or has this project forced you to read him deeper? Or a little bit of both?

PELAN: For me, Lafferty is one of those authors that you can re-read endlessly like James Branch Cabell, Harlan Ellison, Ramsey Campbell, James P. Blaylock, Jack Vance, Michael Shea, Ernest Bramah, Harvey Jacobs and so on.

JRO: Did you ever meet Lafferty? If so, what are your personal impressions of the man?

PELAN: No, and it's likely just as well. The picture of Lafferty that I had built up in my head based on his remarks was a far cry from the reality. In numerous interviews he refers to himself as an ex-drinker, whereas from what I've heard, he was usually blasted out of his mind at most conventions. As an ex-drunk myself, I have no problem at all with folks drinking to excess, but when someone repeatedly claims a sobriety that they don't have, I find it vastly disappointing.

JRO: You are most closely associated with the horror genre. I have to admit that I had to look you up when I saw your name announced as attached to the Lafferty project. As someone who doesn't often stray into the horror genre, I wasn't familiar with your work. Researching you a bit, though, I found that your small press start included publishing small limited editions of Powers and Blaylock (both of which have notably written theologically-slanted lit like Lafferty) and KSR and others. What is your history with sf/f, both as a professional and as a fan?

PELAN: Well, after many years as a serious collector and reader of the whole spectrum of imaginative fiction I sort of stumbled into publishing almost by accident. I guess that the traditional route might well be writer > editor > publisher. I did it in reverse order and just by happenstance founded the most successful small press ever. After I sold Axolotl Press, I took some time off to figure out what should come next and wound up launching Midnight House. The scene was quite a bit different in the 1990s than it had been ten years earlier when simply announcing a book guaranteed a sell-through. Finally I went to work with Centipede Press and Ramble House where I can focus on the aspects of publishing that I enjoy and eschew the parts that I don't feel strongly about.

JRO: You were obviously interested in science fiction and fantasy and your publishing taste leaned toward those on the fringes like Blaylock. So, some questions: Does this Lafferty project feel like a return to or extension of that early Axolotl Press work? Is there a connection or am I stretching? Somewhat related, it's often said that Lafferty is a genre unto himself. Still, his work, while mostly recognizably sf/f, also has strong horror leanings. (Daniel has recently written of Lafferty as writer of "mystical slashers": http://antsofgodarequeerfish.blogspot.com/2014/04/lafferty-as-writer-of-mystical-slashers.html). How does Lafferty fit into your interest in and broad knowledge of the horror genre? Or doesn't he?

PELAN: Well to start off, horror is (a.) a marketing category used by bookstores and (b.) it's really an emotional response to something. You are stretching when you connect Lafferty to the horror genre. On the other hand, you are spot on in connecting Lafferty to me. I've talked about this before on panels on editing. Basically the concept is this, when you have a free-lance editor who can basically do whatever the hell they want, an astute reader can discern their taste pretty easily and can either follow their work or not as the case may be. I used to say (and still do) that if you buy every book that has my name connected to it, you may not like everything that I've chosen to do, but you'll probably understand my reasons for doing it. R.A. Lafferty is the greatest Axolotl Press author to never be published by Axolotl Press (if you'll recall, at the same time Axolotl was in existence Chris Drumm was doing his Lafferty series. So is Lafferty a horror author and connected to my work in that genre? Not at all. Is Lafferty a "John Pelan author"? Very much so.

JRO: How did you get involved with the Lafferty Collected Stories Project? Was this something that you were actively seeking? Did it come about through your previous relationship with Centipede?

PELAN: Well that's an interesting question, as there isn't a simple answer. I've said for years that Lafferty should have all of his stories collected and on my own, I am just obsessive about "Complete stories of" collections, be it Paul Bowles or J.G. Ballard in one volume, Phillip K. Dick in five volumes or Theodore Sturgeon in thirteen, if it's a complete or best of, I'm buying it. If it's author I like a lot and it doesn't seem that anyone else is going publish them in a manner that I consider suitable, it's pretty good bet that sooner or later, I'll be doing it.

Now the cool thing with Jerad at Centipede is that we have similar tastes in literature and also similar tastes in what can be considered commercially viable for his type of production. Also, over the years I guess I've developed a reputation for not being intimidated by large projects. Starting with the five volume set of Manly Wade Wellman stories that I put together for Night Shade books I've gone on to assemble some five books by different authors that run 1000 pages or thereabouts. The Lafferty project will run 10-12 volumes, and simultaneously I'm putting together a set of Day Keene's detective stories which I'm projecting to be 13 or 14 books when completed (oh yeah, the guy knows mystery and detective fiction too) ;-) and some smaller sets such as Wyatt Blassingame's weird menace stories (7 books), John H. Knox (likely five volumes), Arthur Leo Zagat (at least seven books, probably more) and then a whole bunch of two- and three-volume sets. I'm also in discussions with my favorite sf writer about what will be (if the deal comes off) the biggest single author collection in history.

JRO: Tell us the most embarrassing experience of your life. Okay, you can skip this one if you want.

PELAN: I can't really say too much as the situation has been deemed "classified" but it involved several well-known political figures, the Giant Rat of Sumatra, several juggalos and a group of furries...

JRO: One member of our little group of Lafferty fans really wants to know what your favorite color is. What's your favorite color?

PELAN: I'm guessing that this person has (a.) never met me or (b.) hasn't gone to very many conventions. Suffice it to say I'm only wearing all black until I can find something darker...

LAFFERTY DESERVES A DOCUMENTARY
- *a call to action by Andrew Mass*

No doubt the best time to make a documentary about R.A. Lafferty is yesterday. We'll just have to settle for the next best time then, and begin today. As it happens, I've been researching, organizing and collecting materials for a few months now on just such a project. And I wanted to take this opportunity to invite anyone with an interest or inclination to participate.

Of course, that could mean a lot of different things and I'm open to all of them. If you have a Lafferty related story to tell, I'd love to hear it. If you have any archival materials, photos or film, I'd definitely love to see it. I'm hoping to start scheduling interviews soon and to begin collecting footage. Most of all, I hope this is a project that fans everywhere can feel a part of, as we document Lafferty's place in American literature and bring his writing to the attention of a new generation of readers.

If you have any interest please take a look at my project site (http://laffertydoc.blogspot.com), where I'll be updating progress, and feel free to contact me at akmass@gmail.com. And a special thanks to Rich Persaud for co-organizing this terrific publication and allowing me the opportunity to meet you all.

Andrew Mass is a New York based writer who has worked as a copywriter and creative director in digital advertising for most of the last 15 years. He also had an enjoyable stint at NY Public Radio, and as a financial journalist. Andrew studied China at university and spent 1987 at a college in Nanjing. Sometime in the late '90s he stumbled upon a Lafferty book and has been pleasantly bewildered ever since.

ALOYSIUS ASCENDING
by David Cruces

There is a chamber under the Cassiopeian
starblaze, dimly lit by a smoky candle.
Wolf-brother Aloysius sat here listening to
the roar of cataractic planets. The Howling
Worlds told stories of the Puca, histories
of Astrobe, Ktistec Machines and
Choctaw Giants. All of it was too irresistible
for him to leave unrecorded. He rummaged
through his drawer for a pen and paper
and wrote it all down. Writing
consumed his days and nights, with
only short interruptions to drink beer,
make a sandwich, and gather the
twigs of twilight to throw into
the fireplace for warmth. Unlike other
Loup-garou, Aloysius was a considerate
werewolf and never bothered chasing
and devouring humans.

More than a few persons of the
world took notice of these tales. Unique!
Singular! Original! they proclaimed. And
they were exactly right. They wanted to
know more about him. They learned that
in addition to being a werewolf, he was also an
electrical engineer, World War II veteran,
linguistic aficionado, and lover of books.

Then, on one fateful night, the moon
that he so loved to Howl at shone
a moonbeam down on his very person
and sucked him up into the sky
and stars. Wolf-brother Aloysius's life,
like all living things, came to an end.

But the stories he wrote are still
very much alive. Unique! Original! Singular!
Like truth reflected through midnight mirrors!
they still say after reading the story collections.

Werewolves usually have three shadows,
but Aloysius had nine hundred.
This shadow pack and a few
stray dogs kept those stories. They've read
and re-read them over many years.
Wolf-brother's pack Howls long into the
night in remembrance of him.

David Cruces considers Frog On The Mountain to be the greatest story written by human hands.

AN INSTINCT FOR FRIENDSHIP
by John Owen

*F*innegan and Doll Delancy were no longer alone. There was a comical little drunk with them. It seemed as though he'd materialized gradually; he hadn't been there all at once.

"You are the cutest little man I ever did see," Doll told the little drunk. "We are going to adopt you and you will travel with us, aren't we going to, Finnegan? We are going to go all over the country and live like unobtrusive princes. We will keep it gaudy but not let it get out of hand. We've got a million dollars in a suitcase, and we'll give you all you want, won't we, Finnegan? Will you go with us, little man?"

Although Finnegan realized that the little man was not really drunk, and that he and Doll were, yet he was not alarmed. Finnegan had an instinct for friendship, and he always knew a right man from a wrong one.

—*The Devil is Dead*

"Will you go with us, little man?"

Of course I will.

Asked to contribute something to this zine, I immediately

despaired at ever settling on a theme in time. My first impulse was to write something tongue-in-cheek about how Lafferty was not at all original or unique in his vision of the future. He imagined the same future as the rest of 20th century science fiction, a future in which tobacco smoking is taken for granted and celebrated as a good.

In this original essay, I would take examples from Lafferty's writings, such as a time-traveling Thomas More enjoying far-future stogies and a robot enjoying the same. I would compare these examples to copious other examples from other major sf writers, slowly building my case until you, dear reader, picked up briar and leaf and puffed contentedly, satisfied with the present and optimistic once again about the future. But writing that article would probably get this publication banned from all of the drugstores that would otherwise carry it on its magazine racks next to the comics and science fiction books. Because drugstores, at least near me, no longer carry cigars or any tobacco products. What is that you say? Drugstores no longer carry comics or science fiction either? Surely, the future has failed us. Western Civilization is dying. Again.

What we need at the moment is not a cellar full of tobacco (though surely that would not hurt.) What we need is to press through the current death (just one of many) into resurrection. Those of us living in "The Day After the World Ended" are now tasked with learning how to live and love into the future, in The Day After The Day After the World Ended. What Lafferty saw clearly was that the End of the World is not near. The End has recently passed.

Critic Paul Kincaid has recently written about the exhaustion of science fiction and fantasy. The genre, like our culture, like our world, appears to be in the business of dying every few years:

*T*he problem may be, I think, that science fiction has lost confidence in the future. Or perhaps it would be more accurate to say that it has lost confidence that the future can be comprehended.

It is into this present moment of lost confidence that we witness the rediscovery and resurgence of R.A. Lafferty. And with the rediscovery and resurgence of Lafferty, perhaps we will witness a rediscovery and resurgence of Hope. Kevin Cheek has recently pointed to this:

*A*nd come to think of it, I believe at root that that hope [that humanity (we malodorous worms in the middle, we everylouts) does have what it takes to recover, succeed, and evolve] is the real reason for the breadth of Lafferty's appeal. Yes his wordcraft is amazing and original, yes his play with archetypes and accelerated story development is unique and uniquely fun, yes his way with tall-tales is playful and fun and funny while expressing great depth. However, I think the real resonance most of us find is in his hope (often a cranky hope) for all of us.

And if there is a rediscovery and resurgence of Hope, mayhap Faith (the substance of things hoped for, the evidence of things not seen, i.e. the future) and Love are not far behind.

And the greatest of these is Love.

And so I've found my theme.

It seems to me that Lafferty, like his character Finnegan, had an instinct for friendship. And not just surface friendship, but a deep bringing-into-family friendship. And what's more amazing is that this instinct for friendship is somehow communicated through his writing and infects his readers. Reading Lafferty demands an active community. Try reading a Lafferty story/novel in the presence of someone else. Were you able to refrain from reading aloud, from sharing your joy? If so, you have a special kind of immunity. In my experience, the natural reaction is to read aloud, to enjoy the text together.

This response to Lafferty, evidenced in its drive toward community, has manifested itself several times in the past and is manifesting itself in the present. This zine is not something new. We are following in the path of fans who went before us. Fellow fans who could not help but create something in response to Lafferty.

Daniel Otto Jack Petersen has most recently sent out the call. We would all do well to heed him.

*L*et Us Make Common Cause in the High Hilarity!

Now, the way to look at all this from the perspective of practicing artists is that we may thus see in Lafferty, if we have eyes to see it, a fresh and fruitful WAY FORWARD for culture-making....

Notice this also: Lafferty does often write implicitly or explicitly Christian characters who are 'of the faith', who will be part of renewing the world, fighting its demise. But he usually teams them up with doubters and unbelievers (think of believing Paul and doubting Thomas in *Past Master*; or the secular-liberal members of the Institute of Impure Science and their non-secular-liberal associates who are denied membership because they do not meet the 'minimal decency rule' in *Arrive At Easterwine*). This is a way forward for us all as well. We can continue to have our hot debate about Origins and Ends and the Meaning-in-the-Middle, but we can love, respect, play, joke, and creatively work together with each other all the while.

This cooperative creativity and world-construction is the only kind of response appropriate to Lafferty by anyone who has read him with any amount of depth or sensitivity. His stories move, thrill, and tickle us, yes, but merely being passively 'entertained' or 'amused' is just not a live option that these tales present to us.

Yes and amen.

This creativity and world-construction is, as Daniel has written, cooperative. But not only are we called to work in response, we are just as importantly called to "love, respect, play, joke" cooperatively.

One such instance of this cooperation has been manifest in East of Laughter: An Appreciation of R.A. Lafferty, the Facebook group created by David Cruces. This instance being a cooperation in playfully re-awakening ourselves and others to the joys of Lafferty's fiction (and, following this, the joys of living well and dying well), the fruit of which can be seen in this very 'zine. We will keep it gaudy but not let it get out of hand.

This specific gathering of Lafferty disciples (not the first, not the last) is remarkable in its excellencies. Every one of these men and women is more intelligent and more talented than the last. As one of the least of these, I am humbled to be a part of the company.

My own discovery of Lafferty has been recent. My enthusiasm outpaces my experience. What has been just as pleasant as discovering each new Lafferty story has been discovering Lafferty fandom. Each fellow Lafferty fan that I've interacted with (online only so far) has had "an instinct for friendship." Here is a place within the broader fractured science fiction community that feels like home.

The past year, Lafferty's Centennial, has seen the first volume of the Collected Stories from Centipede Press. There has been an increase in news and talk of Lafferty in the past few years.

This recent proliferation of discussion may seem sudden. Really, it's been a long time coming.

Credit where it is due. Many Lafferty fans have kept interest in the stories alive for several decades now, not letting the broader sf community forget about Lafferty.

Interest and talk have been at a low simmer for many years. The aroma wafted through the rest of the big house just as many of us were at our hungriest. We were exhausted. We had lost confidence.

Now, the soup is ready. Suddenly, the invitation to eat and enjoy has gone out far and wide, even to those of us who never set foot in the kitchen (or, if we did, wrinkled our noses and left in a rude huff.)

Scoundrel that I am, having no part in the preparation, I have now boldly arrived at the feast. Miracle of miracles, the hosts are yet gracious. And somehow there is more of this rich soup than any of us could slurp down in a hundred thousand years.

And the fellowship is lovely, maybe best of all when we're all fighting (it hasn't happened yet but surely it should, no?) And the drink is heady stuff and there seems no end of it.

And there's Soft-Talk Susie in the corner whispering in Kevin's ear as they both slurp up something other than soup. And David and Daniel practicing pentecost, tongues of fire glossing Laffertisms in Japanese while Kenji laughs on. And which one of the Bills is that over there in the space pirate garb? How could it be both of them? There's Mark arm-wrestling Sour John. Wait, what is Jim doing there with that expensive book? Is that Gregorio at that other table explaining the 'minimal decency rule' to Gary all over again? How many times now? And that must be Lissanne on the stairs sketching all the rest. How is she working at all with that man in her lap? Could that be? No, he's dead and dead is dead except when it isn't. Dang, this soup is good. And the company grand.

And though this raucous gathering may never know an end, this poor zine contribution is in desperate need of one.

Blessed be this rum.

End.

John Owen comes home each evening to the golden cliché: the u.n.d; the p.h.; and l. and u.w.; and the s.c. (seven more would have been too many). Just to live is a happy riot. He is well known in the future for having barely succeeded in establishing the Northeast Lafferty League, which has grown to cover the Northeast quadrant of this galaxy. On all of the planets, his name has become a byword for any grand success achieved based on wild enthusiasm coupled with poor planning and lack of any applicable skill set. John blogs infrequently about R.A. Lafferty at http://failingevenbetter.blogspot.com

TO BE CONTINUED?

by John Barach

A guy can dream, can't he? And lo! I dreamed, and in my dream there was a book, and when the book was opened, behold, there went forth men and women of great repute, each seeking readers, each with a story in hand, and each story by the same author, the writer Lafferty.

Only a dream, you say, and that is true. Lafferty is lots of fun. Lafferty is sometimes zany. Lafferty isn't very interested in plot or even in logic. Lafferty is difficult. Lafferty is obscure. And it is one thing to commend Lafferty to your friends and another thing entirely to commend him in a way that bears fruit, that garners him new readers. For that, your word may not be enough. But perhaps the word of others....

Dream the same dream, but substitute the name, and you're not dreaming about the possible future but about the past. I was in a small bookstore somewhere when I spotted it: *The Avram Davidson Treasury*, edited by Robert Silverberg and Grania Davis. I was aware of Davidson, though (and this is the point) I had read only one or two of his stories. What sold me on the book was the name on the cover: Gene Wolfe. For the treasury contained not only what some consider Davidson's best stories but also short introductions by noted authors and editors commending and commenting on these stories. Davidson was interesting, but it was Wolfe handing me Davidson's story that made me reach for my wallet.

Did the *Treasury* lead to a huge Avram Davidson revival?

Maybe not, though several other volumes of his stories did appear shortly afterward. But the idea still seems good to me, and what was good for Davidson may be good for Lafferty too, especially given that some big names in science fiction and fantasy have begun to talk about their appreciation for him.

So who could contribute to *An R. A. Lafferty Treasury*? Surely Neil Gaiman would be willing, and perhaps Gene Wolfe, both having written Lafferty-influenced stories. Robert Reginald introduced Lafferty's *It's Down the Slippery Cellar Stairs*. Michael Swanwick did the same for *Iron Tears*, which Nancy Kress and James P. Blaylock blurbed (and if Blaylock is interested, might Tim Powers also be?). Orson Scott Card included a Lafferty story in his collection, *Masterpieces: The Best Science Fiction of the 20ᵗʰ Century*.

Joseph Green contributed to the 1979 tribute *At the Sleepy Sailor*, as did a writer one might not even think to associate with Lafferty, namely, Fred Chappell, who calls *Past Master* "a big shiny delirious clutter of impulse…. It's a glorious mess, and I for one am willing to put up with the mess for the sake of the glory."

Alan Dean Foster's *Impossible Places* has this dedication: "To the memory of Raphael A. Lafferty, / The elf from Oklahoma, / Who could do things with words that most writers can only do with dreams." Foster and Wolfe both wrote for the Davidson collection. Who else from that treasury might find treasure in this one? Perhaps Kate Wilhelm and Ursula K. LeGuin, both of whom also corresponded with Lafferty at least once.

Other correspondents who are, to my knowledge, still alive? Peter Crowther. Ramsey Campbell. James Gunn. Beth Meacham (Tor). Jerry Pournelle. Ian Watson. My guess: If they corresponded with him or, as editors, tried to commission stories from him, they probably liked his work.

And then there's the 1995 Arrell Gibson Lifetime Achievement Award, which Lafferty received upon recommendations by, among others, Brian Attebery, Michael Bishop, Terry Bisson, C. J. Cherryh, Brian Cholfin (Broken Mirrors Press), Jack Dann, Alan Dean Foster, Daniel Knight (United Mythologies Press), Kim Mohan (*Amazing Stories*), Darrell Schweitzer, Michael Swanwick, Harry Turtledove, and Kate Wilhelm.

Who else? John Clute wrote an obituary for Lafferty and, together with Scott Edelman, Robert Silverberg, and Gardner Dozois, composed the board that voted Lafferty the 2002 Cordwainer Smith Foundation "Rediscovery" Award.

Who else? Comb through the blurbs and, for now, count only those writers who are still alive. *Past Master* was blurbed by Samuel R. Delaney ("Marvelously inventive") and Harlan Ellison ("A great galloping madman of a novel, drenched in sound and color"). *Nine Hundred Grandmothers* was blurbed by Ellison again, as well as by Terry Carr ("one of the most original writers in science fiction"). Alexei Panshin blurbed *Fourth Mansions* ("as strange and inventive a book as I have ever read").

Search the web and you'll find accolades and favorable mentions by Mike Resnick, Norman Spinrad, John C. Wright, Michael Flynn, Richard Lupoff, and David Gerrold (who names *Fourth Mansions* as one of the ten books that stayed with him).

Then there are Paul de Filippo and Jonathan Strahan (who says that *Nine Hundred Grandmothers* "meant an enormous amount to me": http://www.litmir.net/br/?b=126152&p=1) and Claude Lalumière ("R.A. Lafferty never ceases to amaze me. His work is always bubbling under the surface when I write, subtly influencing

everything I do. What I learned from Lafferty is somewhat ineffable, as his own work usually is":
http://www.blackgate.com/2011/04/24/an-interview-with-claude-lalumiere-part-two/)

Critics? How about Brian Atteberry, George Slusser, Kathleen Spencer, and Gary K. Wolfe, the latter of whom says that Lafferty "may put people off with his jokey style, but he completely reinvented SF for his own quasi-theological ends and developed a world-view that has yet to be fully explored, or even partially illuminated, by us critics"
(http://www.depauw.edu/sfs/backissues/61/unjustneglect61.htm).

Might there be others? Why not? What about Howard Waldrop or even Eliot Fintushel, both of whom get compared to Lafferty at times? Who else was inspired by him? Who read something by him for the first time just now and can't wait to tell others? And what about … ?

Well, who do you have in mind? Perhaps your name is in this list. Perhaps you're thinking of someone else who could have been included. Perhaps you're just thinking that whoever is included, you'd like to help to make this *Treasury* not just a dream but a reality. Perhaps there should be an address to which you could at least express your interest: LaffertyTreasury@gmail.com. (Aha! So easy is the first step.)

To be continued? We hope so. The only question is: Where will the next rock be?

John Barach (http://barach.us) is the Pastor of Covenant Presbyterian Church in Sulphur, Louisiana. All day at work, he is surrounded by books and yet he still brings more home from the library several times a week.

UP CLOSE, AND IN PARTICULAR
by Martin Heavisides

How much can be said in how little by a seasoned adept at multum in parvo? Consider in this context two repeated phrases that occur at a distance of two hundred thirty pages from each other (in the Dobson hardcover edition of *Fourth Mansions*):

> *J*im Bauer, as a matter of fact, did not kill himself that day. Neither did he kill Arouet Manion. The sickly fear of death that was on Arouet added a curious and glittering element to the weave. Imagine a man being afraid of a little thing like dying, a mutated man at that. But cowardice might be as necessary an element as arrogance and dishonesty and hatred to make a weave really work.
>
> Bauer postponed his own death for a while, regretfully, as he believed there was still much work to be done in generating the weave and he believed he could do it better in the body. Later, later he would do it.
>
> But he did enlist an actual demon named Baubo to join the weave. This expanded the membership to nine. We will see how it works, we will see how it works.
>
> *Fourth Mansions*, pp. 115-116

And Bauer was letting go, though his fingers
throbbed out blood from the intensity of his
grip on the iron railing. One by one, the
members broke him out of the weave. Letitia
Alive arose from a couch in an interior room,
the hypnosis over her broken. She walked out
of the house Morada and into the road. She had
no resemblance to Letitia Bauer now, and no
remembrance of the several days she had
spent in Morada. Completely confused, back as
the girl she had been before she was mind-
napped, she walked away down the front road.
She left the weave. She had never been in it
strongly.

Letitia Dead found release in the cleansing of
the weave and felt the first joy since she had
died. And Hondo (why such a thing, why such a
thing?) was throwing the weave to Fred Foley,
as soon as Bauer could be broken out of it.

Fourth Mansions, pp 245-246

I won't attempt to fill in the wider context of the novel, even if
that were possible in less than 252 richly intricate pages—why
should I deny you the personal pleasure of discovering for yourself
the patricks, the falcons, the hydra headed brain weave and the
recurring race of meddlers who live on for aeons, skipping from
body to body? All you need to know about these passages is that
both concern the hydra-headed brain-weave, which attempts (well,
doesn't every protagonist in this novel?) to shape to its own end
the present and future destiny of humanity. In passage 1 Jim Bauer,
probably the most evil and certainly most self-satisfied of the
seven persons who incited the weave, has control—he thinks in

perpetuity; in the second he is broken out of the weave and Fred
Foley is given control of it—one of two unwelcome gifts Foley is
given in these hectic final pages. Each turns on the fulcrum of a
reiterated phrase. The meaning of each phrase in context is partly
in the words, but much more in the similarity and difference of the
rhythms. "We will see how it works, we will see how it works."
"Why such a thing, why such a thing?"

Each iteration has two accented syllables, but the rhythms
differ: "We will see how it works" is anapest, "Why such a thing?"
is trochee-iamb. Why connect them then? First, because each is the
key phrase in a passage about the brain-weave; second, because
each is in the direct voice of the point-of-view character; third,
because each phrase is ritually or rhetorically repeated. (Still, the
truncated echo is so muffled it's unsurprising to me how many
close readings of this novel it took before I noticed it.) How much
does each phrase tell us about the character of each implied
speaker?

Anapest is often a rollicking, even unsettling cadence,
sometimes a sonorous one. In the context of Bauer's placidly
homicidal musings (cold and slow-moving as the blood in a
reptile's veins) it reeks of smug complacency (redoubled by the
self-congratulatory repetition, which also indicates Bauer's
conviction that no possible change in the weave could ever cause it
to slip from his sovereign control). The fact that this is the one
sentence clearly in Jim Bauer's voice (and in the first person
plural) implicates the reader and is likeliest to produce a recoil of
revulsion.

Trochee-iamb is a rhythm that recoils on itself, and must
indicate at least serious misgivings, especially if instantly and
jerkily repeated. Partly because he's sampled Jim Bauer's otiose
reflections and the barely governable passions of the others in the
weave, partly because he's being tested to the maximum in every

direction at once, he is terrifically (doubly) reluctant to accept control of the weave (with the best will in the world, can it be controlled?), even when it's thrown to him by probably the best, certainly the least self-satisfied member of it. He has nothing of the dubious self-mastery of Jim Bauer, little but doubt that he has mastery of the mounting self-contradictions in his own nature—which is why, perhaps, he is the only one alive who might in his very person untangle the intricate conundrum of the weave—not to mention the roiling, perturbed world at large.

All this is not implicit only in these ritual phrases, the latter a refracted echo of the former, but the context within which each is set like a jewel would be infinitely diminished without them, as would the echo and resonance between the two passages. A matter of mere style then? By no means. Mere style is a formal filigree designed to conceal an absence; style this resonant is a sounding of the height and breadth and depth of a vivid presence.

HILLARY ARDRI AND JANE CHANTAL ARDRI

Illustration by Lydia Petersen

*O*ne thing I know is that a happy computer can work wonders, and that a computer is most happy when it can indulge itself in a little bit of sociability. But computers don't find the society of humans all that captivating. Some computer-owners stable a goat with each computer to keep it from getting lonesome. That's the second best solution to the problem. But the best solution is to let the computer welcome the guest of its choice, and most computers are kept too clean and antiseptic by their owners to appeal to the special visitors. But I was never bothered by the fetish of cleanliness and over-maintenance. My computer has a poltergeist friend that lives in its maw and does not take up any physical space there. And my computer is happy by this circumstance. So it works wonders for me.

R. A. Lafferty, *East of Laughter* (1988, Morrigan Publications, pp. 5-6)

THE EPIC OF MAN AND HIS FRIENDS
OR
SLUMMING IT WITH THE ONTIC OUTCASTS
OR
MAY OUR EYES BE BIG ENOUGH TO TAKE IN THE NINE HUNDRED PERCENT GAIN IN EVERYTHING!

by Daniel Otto Jack Petersen

There is a conspiracy, carried on by humans and associates-of-humans and directed by principalities and powers, to reject vast areas of the world and to paint them over with little black brushes to make them look like no more than cracks. Well, I know ways to oppose that conspiracy and to lead many people out of the narrow and mundane desert and into the interdicted green meadows.

-Raphael Aloysius Lafferty, "The Man Who Walked Through Cracks" (1978)

Wyman's overpopulated universe is in many ways unlovely. It offends the aesthetic sense of us who have a taste for desert landscapes, but this is not the worst of it. Wyman's slum of possibles is a breeding ground for disorderly elements.

-Willard Van Orman Quine, "On What There

Is" (1953)

> *Barnaby insisted… "I am believing that no creatures have ever stopped happening, but some of them have stopped being apparent. This calls into question the whole nature of reality."*
>
> *"What doesn't," Harry O'Donovan said.*
>
> -R. A. Lafferty, "And Read the Flesh Between the Lines" (1974)

> *How many possible men are there in that doorway?*
>
> -W. V. O. Quine, "On What There Is" (1953)

Introduction: Fear of a Bloated Universe

Once there were two philosophers who debated each other about the nature of reality. Their Lafferty-esque names were Willard Van Orman Quine and Alexius Meinong. (The latter is dubbed "Wyman" in Quine's essay quoted above.) These two were real men from the 20th century. On that much, at least, I think they agreed. But after that common ground, they disagreed sharply about what else was real, or indeed, what *could possibly* be real.

If Lafferty did not know of Quine's influential essay "On What There Is" (1948), then he surely must have felt its influence by other channels, for Lafferty's life work looks almost wholly devoted to refuting the ontological disposition behind Quine's paper. (Ontology is the study of what kinds of entities actually exist.) That disposition is rooted in what is known as Occam's

Razor, a term Lafferty explicitly cited in a number of stories, most famously "Thus We Frustrate Charlemagne" (1967). It is the idea that one needs to be very strictly sure to posit the existence of no more entities in the world than are absolutely necessary – and the fewer the better. Though it can be useful, there is often a current of fear that runs through the implementation of this intellectual attitude. Quine's disgust and anxiety are palpable in the quote from his paper above. Not only does he find an open ontology aesthetically "unlovely", he worries about ontological overpopulation and the resultant metaphysical slums that become a "breeding ground for disorderly elements". Sprinkled throughout his paper are further complaints of the "rank luxuriance" of the "bloated universe" his philosophical opponent posits, with its "occult entities" so hard to nail down with tight criteria of existence. So Quine's essay recommends the usual xenophobic programme for unwanted ghettos: "I feel we'd better simply clear Wyman's slum and be done with it."

Suffice it to say that, as regards this ontological disposition, Lafferty preferred to slum it with the ontic outcasts. Indeed, from stories like "Guesting Time" (1965) and "Ishmael into the Barrens" (1971), it is clear that Lafferty was not one to worry overmuch about overpopulation. His concern was depopulation.

Cornucopious Collections and Ridiculous Mnemonics

Now even though he is known as one of the wildest and most reality-bending authors to ever write, you also really can't get *earthier* than Lafferty. He exhibits a deep pleasure in the physical objects that surround us, and he delights to catalogue them for us in vivid and vast array. It is the point and pleasure of this essay to show Lafferty again and again exhibiting this habit of cataloguing everything he can lay his attention on, from the common to the arcane to the bizarre, and then to show something of his theological underpinnings for that frame of mind and practice.

It is fascinating to note that Lafferty's wide-angle and deeply layered view of physical existence bears some similarity to the vision advocated by a recent philosophical movement known as "object-oriented ontology" (OOO). Graham Harman's writings on OOO, for example, are often replete with rhapsodic lists of non-human objects, which serve as vivid reminders of the physical surfaces and entities that surround, uphold, and impinge on every one of us during every single second of every single day – and also of more remote entities that yet share this universe with us. Lafferty's writing has a habit of frequently and lavishly enumerating such lists as well. The exuberance and excess of his much-remarked Tall Tale style is at play in the sheer length and erudition of the lists, quite literally topping and outdoing any similar sort of list I've ever seen by another writer.

Take, for example, the collector Leo Nation in Lafferty's story "All Pieces of a River Shore" (1971). We are told:

> *H*e collected old pistols, old ball shot, grindstones, early windmills, walking-horse threshing machines, flax combs, Conestoga wagons, brass-bound barrels, buffalo robes, Mexican saddles, slick horn saddles, anvils, Argand lamps, rush holders, hay-burning stoves, hackamores, branding irons, chuck wagons, longhorn horns, beaded serapes, Mexican and Indian leatherwork, buckskins, beads, feathers, squirrel-tail anklets, arrowheads, deerskin shirts, locomotives, streetcars, mill wheels, keelboats, buggies, ox yokes, old parlor organs, blood-and-thunder novels, old circus posters, harness bells,

> Mexican oxcarts, wooden cigar-store Indians,
> cable-twist tobacco a hundred years old and
> mighty strong, cuspidors (four hundred of
> them), Ferris wheels, carnival wagons, carnival
> props of various sorts, carnival proclamations
> painted big on canvas. Now he was going to
> collect something else.

A typical reaction for me, when reading such a list from Lafferty, is to feel both awe and laughter as the erudition mounts and mounts. The bristling list is a vivid, rolling history of physical arcana—mostly regional, mechanical, and of human manufacture, but often of the sort that involves the local ecology's fauna and flora (buffalo and squirrels and deer, hay and flax and tobacco) and is also inclusive of cultural productions (novel, circus, carnival). The unrolling sensation, as if we're watching these items reel by us one by one, matches the story's central conceit of collecting old carnival river-shore panoramas that used to be unreeled on rolls before the eyes of paying observers. And it is a sensation often repeated in Lafferty.

Take for another example the alternate history of Lafferty's "Assault On Fat Mountain" (1976) where a differently carved USA than the one we know is envious of its rich neighbours, the Free Nation of Appalachia. A rabble-rouser in that alternate USA is making his case for a move against their wealthy neighbour-nation by means of a high-piled and "cornucopious" (Lafferty's word elsewhere in the story) list intended to salivate the tongues and grumble the bellies of his hearers:

> Consider the wealths in High Appalachia: the
> red grapes of Roane and the white grapes of
> Smokey Mountain Vineyards; the sweet corn
> centers of fertile Shelby, and the popcorn

plantations of Cumberland; the flax, the wool, the cotton, the Jim-pie-weed cloth; the peat and the coal and the pine-knots for fuel; the rock oil from the hills and the catfish oil from the streams; the pumpkin bread, the hickory nut bread, the bean bread every day of the week; fat beef, fat pork, fat mutton; ducks and geese and woodcock and savanna hen; turkey and guinea; the plump rabbits of Ozarkia and the meaty woodchucks of Doniphan; light wheat, dark rye, barley, and rolling fields of oats; sunflower seeds, pecans and peanuts. Would it be robbery if we took our fair share of these things, nor waited for their niggardly food trains?

This list is more focused, an agricultural panorama of the region; but it is testimony not only to Lafferty's erudition, but also his sheer fascination with a wide array of non-human material entities that shore up human existence.

These lists can seem to come in quite off-handedly as well, and in even quirkier erudition and array. Toward the very beginning of his Hugo-award-winning story "Eurema's Dam", Lafferty has a hilarious and richly ecological way of showing how his allegedly dull-witted protagonist learned things the slow and hard way:

When, about the middle of his ninth year, Albert made a breakthrough at telling his right hand from his left he did it by the most ridiculous set of mnemonics ever put together. It had to do with the way dogs turn around before lying down, the direction of whirlpools and whirlwinds, the side a cow is milked from and a horse is mounted from, the direction of twist of oak and sycamore leaves, the maze patterns of rock moss and tree moss, the cleavage of limestone, the direction of a hawk's wheeling, a shrike's hunting, and a snake's coiling (remembering that the Mountain Boomer is an exception), the lay of cedar fronds and balsam fronds, the twist of a hole dug by a skunk and by a badger (remembering pungently that skunks sometimes use old badger holes). Well, Albert finally learned to remember which was right and which was left, but an observant boy would have learned his right hand from his left without all that nonsense.

This list is wonderful for its simultaneous scope and focus. The scope is that the items are drawn from a wide regional sweep and purport to exhibit specialist knowledge, and the focus is that each and every one of the items is included in the list because it exhibits something directional in its texture or behaviour. The lesson we might garner from Albert's "ridiculous" memory aids here strikes me as similar to what explorers learn in Lafferty's celebrated Camiroi stories (collected in *Nine Hundred Grandmothers*): you have to become a little stupider before you become smarter. On the planet Camiroi, this is partly by learning to read books a *lot* slower, at a pace we would call severely remedial. Lafferty is poking fun at his protagonist in "Eurema", but he is secretly poking fun at us too, that we learn basic things like our right from our left all too hastily and easily. Here too we need to slow down our "reading", but this time it is for the sake of correcting our woeful illiteracy of our environment.

As the few references to smell above attest, Lafferty brings in encounter with non-human objects through all the senses. In

"Condillac's Statue, or Wrens In His Head" (1970), a few French philosophers invest a stone statue with a mind and the normally inanimate object thus begins to engage the world, sense by sense, beginning with smell:

> *L*athered horses, foam-whitened harness, green goop in the horse trough, those were smells of the little park and the big country. Wet flintstones, grackle birds and the mites on them; river grass and marl grass and loam grass; oaks and chestnuts, wagon-wheel grease, men in leather; stone in shade, and stone in sun; hot mules, and they do *not* smell the same as hot horses; mice in the grass roots, muskiness of snakes; sharpness of fox hair, air of badger holes; brown dust of the Orleans road, red dust of the road to Chateau-dun; crows that have fed today, and those who have not; time-polished coach wood; turtles eating low grapes, and the grapes being bruised and eaten; sheep and goats; cows in milk, new stilted colts; long loaves, corks of wine bottles, cicadas in pigweeds; hands of smiths and feet of charcoal burners; whetted iron on travelers; pungent blouses of river men; oatcakes and sour cream; wooden shoes, goose eggs, new-spread dung, potato bugs; thatchers at work; clover, vetch, hairy legs of bumblebees. There are no two of these things that have the same smell... He stood and smelled for a month, and the smells informed his stone.

Again, a wonderfully erudite list of regional and historical objects and phenomena (the story is set in 18th century France, just before the French Revolution), some of them odd to think of having a distinct smell for (the mites on birds, "sharpness of fox hair", "hairy legs of bumblebees", etc.). You get the sense that these lists are severely truncated. They could go on indefinitely. Lafferty's is a very, very full world, and yet, as he often likes to reiterate, it is not overcrowded. These are not really slums. This is rampant life.

A Flagstone Cries Out

Speaking of the sensing of stones, Lafferty is at times perfectly willing to take an object's-eye-view of the history of the human and the non-human. In "From The Thunder Colt's Mouth" (collected in In the *Wake of Man: A Science Fiction Triad*, Bobbs-Merrill, 1975), a novella about an ontic struggle for which version(s) of history will obtain, we are told of stones in an opera house that can not only remember all of the venue's performances from the past, but can also recall the emanations of their fellow objects from the opera house's past. This generates yet another erudite, catalogued history of objects that we often take for granted:

> *T*he gimcrack stones have the glow of every wax candle or rush light that ever lighted the performing house; they have the hot-wax smell, the rush-fat smell, the evocative rag-wick stench. They have the glittering and guttering of the bear oil, the whale oil, the lard lamps. They have the whispering sound and flicker of old illuminating gas flames, the garishness of the limelights and the carbide lights, the later and stronger shine of the electrical chandeliers and of the mercury spotlights. Ah, do any of you remember the unearthly whiteness of the

old sodium lights? The stones will remember it.
(page 35)

Again we have the meshing of various kinds of the non-human:
the refracted elements of light and fire together with the various
smells of materials that come from bees, bears, whales, and animal
fat in general.

Then we are told of a certain flagstone in the street outside the
opera house that persisted through the street's changes, from slates
to cobbles to bricks to asphalt, and which still remembers the
history of vehicles that went over it:

> *I*t remembers the underbellies of thousands of
> horses and carriages that stomped and
> rumbled over it. Ah, what great horse vehicles
> those were! Who now living, except possibly
> our host Duffey, remembers them all? The
> Acme Royal Top and the Acme Open, the
> Southern Beauty, the Fulton Road Cart, the
> Livery Special, the Farmer's Canopy Top Surrey,
> Johnson's Jump-Seat Buggy, the Imperial
> Carriage, Dempster's Three-Spring Handy
> Wagon, Drexel's Eight-Horse Dray, Pontiac's
> Special Milk Wagon, Hallock's Grocery Cart, the
> Sears Famous, the Road Runner. Ah, I see
> brimming eyes at the mention of these things.
> The fragrance of road apples will always be a
> primary part of nostalgia. (page 36)

I'm not sure what Lafferty is doing here with the fictionalized
names of pre-automobile vehicles, but the general point of objects
remembering is what we're after for now. In keeping with
Lafferty's characteristic upping of the oddity, we then go from

invented arcane names of old vehicles to the even quirkier (and no doubt equally fictional) names of various brands of whips that drove the animals that pulled those old vehicles, and the attendant sounds of such traffic:

That stone in Decatur Street remembers the quickening snap and bang of whips... and their airy swishing. Ah, the Cowles Buggy Whip: we shan't see its like again! The Jacksonville Drover, the S.R. and Co.'s Australian, the Western Mule Skinner, the Milford Quirt, Hodson's Superior Horse Whip, the San Antonia, the Fancy, the Never-Break Dog Whip, the Elko. What days do these not bring back! The cursing wagoners, the rattling of whiffletrees, the jangle of even-chains! Some of these things still live in the blessed place, and others have been cut down by the weed-hacker. (pages 36-37)

Rounding out this passage, the stone's-eye-view recalls yet another, and later, era of vehicles passing over it:

The stone remembers the underside of old streetcars. It even remembers the round punchings of old streetcar transfers wafting down on the easy breeze, and the odor of trolley ozone. It remembers the underside of every automobile that ever went down Decatur Street, and we dare not roll their names off our tongue lest nostalgic riots ensue. The stone recalls faithfully every two-legged and four-legged walker of the street. And it remembers, from the underside also, the jeweled sky of

eighty thousand nights. It's a very talkative old
stone, and it is talking to our experts and their
instruments at this moment. (page 37)

In the penultimate sentence of this last list we enter truly into a
glimpse of a non-human perspective: the rock's view of the
intermittent night sky as the vehicles rode endlessly over it. It
resonates with OOO theory's emphasis on non-human objects
encountering other non-human objects and on all objects being
inexhaustible in their being. Take, for example, a passage where
the philosophy of Alfred North Whitehead (another real
philosopher with a Lafferty-esque name) is being explicated:

An actual entity such as a star is the site of
innumerable forces, the locus of an absolute
effect mirrored in all other beings. But other
entities do not encounter the star in quite this
way. Rocks, comets, plants, and humans each
"objectify" the star differently, encounter it in
some specific and limited way that does not
exhaust the full of its reality. (Graham Harman,
2010, *Towards Speculative Realism: Essays and
Lectures*, Zero Books, page 38)

Stones encounter stars differently than we do. Lafferty's
flagstone perspective of all that rolls over it through the centuries
is a wonderful encounter with alien consciousness, right here on
the taken-for-granted ground of our own historical world. Notice
that the non-human object is "faithful" to the plenitude of history
even as some humans in this tale try to mow down the richness of
the past (hence, the reference to the "weed-hacker" in the list
before this). One can't help but feel an allusion to the rocks being
ready to cry out should humans remain silent in the New Testament
Gospels.

The Experience of Planet-Fall is a Daily Thing

Lafferty loved to spin yarns of extra-terrestrial contact. His "planet-fall" stories (e.g. "Nine Hundred Grandmothers", "Snuffles", "Name of the Snake", "World Abounding", "Once On Aranea") are some of his most memorable and celebrated (and there are some spectacular lesser known ones as well, such as "Smoe and the Implicit Clay" and "Thieving Bear Planet"). Yet Lafferty saw aliens right here in the terrestrial realm that most of us miss. As he writes in his essay "The Case of the Moth-eaten Magician":

*T*o me, most of the great moments of science fiction are planet-falls: unshipping and setting foot on new worlds. And yet the experience of planet-fall is a daily thing, one that never grows stale. It happens a dozen or a hundred times a day. We live on a tolerably new world, and there is always the feeling of having just arrived on it. This is a world that is always more than ninety percent unexplored by ourselves, and we have a compulsion to get on with the exploration. It's an intricate and massive world, prodigious in detail and almost beyond numbering in its dimensions; compendious, encyclopedic, physically astonishing, prodigal in line and color, alive on a dozen different levels, of great friendliness and affection in most of its fauna and especially in its "superior fauna" known as mankind. This species is more delightful than all the tribbles and fuzzies that can be imagined. This world, probably a masterwork among worlds, is loaded with encounters and happenings; and do not forget that etymologically all happenings are happy. (*Fantastic Lives: Autobiographical Essays By Notable Science Fiction Writers*, 1981, edited by Martin H. Greenburg, Southern Illinois University Press, pages 58-59)

With a view of the world like this, it's no wonder Lafferty's work is replete with these wide-ranging lists that are almost hyper-aware of the non-human (but not to the neglect of the fascinating humans themselves, as he says above; indeed, it is no accident that Lafferty evinces a celebrated wide-angle sympathetic gaze as regards ethnicity and culture as well, most notably in his many attractive Native American characters).

Lafferty also often chronicles how we miss these daily planet-falls. In "All But the Words" (1971), a group experiments with translation between species, with the hope of "instant distant translation" with cosmically far-flung extraterrestrials:

*T*he translation devices themselves would be adequate for ordinary work. They could now interpret roughly the thought processes of earthworms and ferns and even crystals. They could record and even verbalize the apprehensions of metals under stress, and, to an extent, the group consciousness of gathering thunderheads. Any language, terrestrial or distant, could be given a cogent interpretation. But something more was required.

Again, the offhand way that Lafferty introduces profound leaps into the imagined possibilities of non-human consciousness are breath-taking. I have savoured these sentences many times over, just revelling in the piquant xenophilic empathy of the ideas: thought processes of earthworms and crystals! And the real effort to jump from human familiarity into the non-human: I will never again look at a bridge, for example, without thinking about the stress the steel may be under. Nor will I look at dark clouds piling up in preparation for a storm without wondering "what are you guys thinking about up there?" And this is part of Lafferty's programme: to raise human consciousness by lateralizing it into non-human consciousness, making us aware that, in one sense or another, all things are "aware", that we exist within an ontological community far, far larger and wider than we are wont to notice. This is a project dear also to OOO theorists, though their philosophical underpinnings and outcomes, in some central ways, will be different from Lafferty's.

As the tale of "All But the Words" proceeds, Lafferty brings in some wise judgment on the ironies of our search for contact with extra-terrestrial minds:

> *R*apport is what we want, and we don't have it. We can study the dragonfly, but are we ever really concerned with the dragonfly's concern for his family? We don't really like the monstrous miniatures. We've no sympathy with the terrified arrogance of the arachnid; how can we have sympathy for really strange creatures? How can we talk to an alien if we don't even like to talk to our own kind?

That empathy is what makes us human is a recurring theme in science fiction, most famously in Philip K. Dick's *Do Androids Dream of Electric Sheep?*, where empathy with animals in particular is taken as a sure sign of our humanity. Such concerns are rendered in characteristically Laffertian tone here, pushing onward from empathy into downright sympathy, causing us to gasp and chuckle both, the wonder and the humour blending into a surprise condemnation of the xenophobia right under our noses. (I note that, though Lafferty's fairly consistent symbology requires him to usually give short shrift to spiders and a few other species, such as snakes and cats, it is gratifying to see here a good word for the creepy little arachnids. His symbology with animals and monstrosity is yet another area I hope to deal with in a later article.)

Sure, Lafferty's using anthropomorphism, but he's using it weirdly and wisely, in a fashion that undermines misleading anthropocentric tendencies. As the Anglican scholar, Richard Bauckham, has pointed out about animal poetry in the Bible, some degree of anthropomorphism is actually necessary and desirable. Drawing on the work of cognitive ethologist Marc Bekoff, Bauckham notes: "only by means of anthropomorphism have we any means at all of empathy with other conscious creatures". Hence, eschewing at least some cautious, biocentric anthropomorphism is actually dangerous:

> *R*enouncing anthropomorphism altogether is bound to be reductionist, explaining animal behaviour in wholly mechanistic terms. To use anthropomorphic language need not imply that we recognise no difference between our own feelings and those of animals; only that we postulate something similar on the basis of the behaviour we observe. For the horse to feel excitement and pleasure cannot be the same as for us to do so; but it is reasonable to suppose the horse experiences something of the sort: horse-excitement and horse-pleasure. Bekoff

argues for the scientific use of
anthropomorphism provided it is used carefully
and "biocentrically", meaning that we make
every attempt to understand who animals are in
their own world. (*Bible and Ecology:
Rediscovering the Community of Creation*, 2010,
Darton, Longman and Todd, page 53)

Horse-excitement and horse-pleasure are ideas I think Lafferty could have gotten behind. Of course, Bauckham notes that ancient biblical poetry will not have been "scientific", but that still, the biblical writers "stay close to the animal's observed behaviour": "They respect the mystery of other beings, while treating them as subjects with awareness and feelings akin to some of our own." Precisely what we see Lafferty doing here, I think. "This cautious degree of anthropomorphism is very important for human relationships with other animals. It enables us to recognise them as subjects of their own lives and not mere objects for human use" (ibid.). This digression about anthropomorphism is actually crucial to understanding what Lafferty does with animals, I think. I plan to delve further into Lafferty's more focused excursions into the Animal Other in the next article. Let us simply note here that Lafferty ends the above passage about sympathy for the dragonfly and spider with a rather damning question (and note how equates "our own kind" with the larger ecological community of Earth, not just fellow humans). The question Lafferty's story asks of us shows us we are not ready for extra-terrestrial alien contact until we welcome *terrestrial* alien contact. (And the rest of 'All But the Words' plays this out in a way that is highly amusing and sobering at once.)

An Incredible Advance in the Seeing Adventure ("I Love Alien Encounter")

This widening of vision that Lafferty advocates will, for him, go far beyond a richer sympathy with the ecology and the "inanimate" environment, but it is not less than this. Indeed, he imagines in "Make Sure the Eyes Are Big Enough" (1982) that the animals might well end up ahead of the humans in acquiring a truly and incredibly larger vision of existence. In this story it is the "giggling cows" that kick off the quantum upgrade in sight, which now includes a "nine-tenths of the world", the "Big Circus", that we have heretofore been blind to:

> *T*here was an incredible advance and expansion in the seeing adventure, that's what it was. There had never been anything like it for a long, long time. When medium-early man had suddenly acquired color-vision and so moved out of the old black-and-gray dinginess, that must have been something of the same explosive and emerging experience.

This nine-tenths of the world, in the story, has been blind to the existence of humans as well, though they had heard of us: "You are creatures out of mythology!" the fish-faced and reptilian-faced (and things of weirder aspect: "quasi-human, way-off-human, and comically and rampantly animal") delightedly exclaim when they see the humans. A "fine-looking, rubbery, frog-faced person" among them expresses the attitude Lafferty is agitating for us to genuinely acquire, when the frog-face says simply and frankly: "I love alien encounter."

Stimulating Creature

Illustration by Daniel Otto Jack Petersen
(the back side of the page is Quine's essay, "On What There is")

It came onto him like a big door banging open and letting in endless masses of sunshine and color, all of them inhabited by stimulating creatures... new throngs of creatures, human, quasi-human, way-off-human, and comically and rampantly animal.

-R. A. Lafferty, "Make Sure the Eyes Are Big Enough" (1982)

And where a number of Lafferty's stories end either with bloody death (usually with some hope of resurrection) or with a crisis point reached and the outcome uncertain, this tale ends with the hoped-for enlightenment already taking place, even if humans (the rather bumbling "lords of creation") are a few minutes behind. And it ends on the all-inclusive hope that none be "left out" of the "Big See" that is taking hold worldwide:

> *T*he cows are still giggling their delight in Monaghan's meadow... And so are other things.
>
> Gar-fish are giggling in the lakes. Honker geese are giggling in their skies and in their swamps. Earthworms are giggling in the ground, and squirrels are chortling in the hickory trees.... The Fish-and-Game Department guys are reporting happier species by the hour.
>
> It is a many-fronted chemical advent, a world-wide movement. It has come to the gophers in their tunnels. It will come even to the lords of creation very soon, maybe even to the rest of them today. And when it comes, it will be a nine hundred percent gain in everything. May our eyes be big enough to take it all in! Don't let any of us be left out.
>
> What's that funny noise in the front yard?
>
> It's giggling moles tearing up the ground. But they are seeing the "Big See" too.

Weaving the Seamless Garment – Down There at Whale Town

Now all this wide-angle way of seeing in Lafferty keeps trying to "add up" to some kind of Big Picture, and that adding up is always embattled, opposed by those who want to deny that there is any such Big Picture, or at least that it doesn't take the shape Lafferty's Catholicism says it does. You can see this debate in the incredibly eco-rich and peculiar novel *Serpent's Egg* (1987), which I hope to talk more about in the next article. Despite being his single most animal-profuse novel, its theme is more to do with inward psychological depths than beings outside of us. Yet Lafferty draws no disjunction between inner ecologies and outer ecologies. He urges that we need to get both of those houses in order (a wild order, to be sure) and then we need to get them synchronised again in fruitful ferocity (or ferocious fruitfulness, if you prefer).

At one point in *Serpent's Egg* there is a discussion in progress about what the goal of existence is and a character called Felix Snake-and-Dove is saying:

> We are here to weave the seamless garment of our individual lives, and of the lives of those around us, of the neighborhood, of the countryside, of all the creatures down to the smallest, of all realms and continents and oceans. We are here to weave the seamless garment that will be highly detailed from the subatomic particles to the galaxy clusters. It must include all minds and ideas and inklings, all joys and all immediacies. There can never be enough weavers, there can never be enough brilliant details in the seamless garment known

as "The Life Affair". And we can never be finished with it, for it continues to grow seamlessly.

But this is countered by another character:

"**W**eaving is outmoded, Felix," said Livius Secundus the history-writing Computer. "Fabrics are no longer woven. Now they are extruded by extruding machines. Personal groups, landscapes, worlds, galaxies, all are extruded by a simple extruding machine which you could make yourself."

Whatever the fine details about weaving vs. extruding in terms of technology and manufacture, and how these might operate here symbolically, it is clear in the novel (and in Lafferty's body of work as a whole) that Lafferty favours the first view expressed and finds the latter somehow reductively mechanistic.

Later in *Serpent's Egg*, such a grand weaving begins to take very strange shape: whales are using deep-sea lice to sculpt a megalithic undersea mosaic out of multi-coloured marble. If that's not weird enough, this "ocean" has formed recently in the middle of Oklahoma! (It's really a dream ocean, but this is only half explicit.) This may sound just a little too 'out there' for you, but don't worry, Lafferty reassures us: "It was utterly strange down there at Whale Town, and completely homey also. A sign which the whales had put up proclaimed to all visitors 'We're Glad You're Here'."

Feel at home? You probably won't for long as the description ensues:

*T*he beautiful pink, lilac, tan, orange, and mauve-tinted marble of the Whales' Constructions had also on it happy blotches and gouts of the greenest green ever [...] "The Green of Swarming, Ocean-floor etching, deep-sea lice". [...] The small ocean-lice were etching figures and faces into the big marble and granite stone-pillars. Though not one, and not ten thousand of the little lice had enough scope and reach to comprehend what they were sculpting, to know what the statuary was all about, yet the lice were receiving and obeying orders from somebody, and likely from the whales. The portraiture art, cut in high-and-bas relief out of the giant stone pillars and walls and lintels, had to be the Art of the Whales.

Mostly the faces and forms were those of famous whales of yore. But there were also distinguished-looking animal faces, human faces, god faces, even strange computer faces, all emerging from the big stones that the sea-lice were sculpting for the whales. And whenever they finished one of the great and distinguished faces, the sea-lice covered it over with a beautiful and thin plating of nacre or mother-of-pearl. (pages 137-38)

Notice the ontologically all-inclusive scope of this epic sculpture series: computers, gods, animals, and humans. Faces emerging from the total formation of the many details was an image Lafferty returned to, as we'll see below. Indeed, it was something he said of his own body of work, which he claimed formed an unfinished and unrealised whole, a face that never quite materialised. This characterisation of his own oeuvre is consistent with his conception of ontological weaving above: "we can never be finished with it, for it continues to grow seamlessly".

Indeed, it's humorous to note that Lafferty appears to be absolutely bursting with a proliferation of erudite lists of the non-human. After the undersea sculpture passages above, Lafferty seems to have an overflow to which he simply must give expression. It was "gala", he tells us, for the "Nations of the Fishes" who "flocked" to this spot in Oklahoma "on the sea-rumor" of a new ocean:

> So there were fishes from all the far Oceans, Paddle-Fishes and Sturgeons, Garpikes and Bowfins, Ocean Carp, Suckers, Ocean Catfish, Herrings, Trout, Salmons, Tarpons, Whitefishes, Pikes, Eels and Conger Eels, Sticklebacks, Pipefishes, Seahorses, Silver-Sides, Mullets, Spinny-Rays, Sea-Basses, Bluefish, Porcupine Fishes, Remoras, Anglers, Mackerels, Swordfishes, Flounders, Codfishes. Red-Snappers, Lungfish, Alligator-Gar, Salt-Water Dogfish, the Stomias Boa. Starfish and Squids. Oh, the Sharks! The Dogfish Sharks, the Great White Sharks, the Sand Sharks, the Hammerhead Sharks... The Rays and the Skates and the Swordfish! (pages 138-39)

The Big Picture has not coalesced by the end of the novel, but the spirit of the ending is a "hope-of-the-world thing".

Apes and Angels On Its Fringes (and Ditching the Dismal Desert)

The grandly woven "Life Affair" takes a little more concrete, or rather glass, shape in Lafferty's story "In Deepest Glass: An Informal History of Stained Glass" (1980) – a tale that deserves its own essay (as, really, so many of his stories do). In this story a series of stained glass masterpieces etched by the "living spirits of the weather, the Living Spirits of the world" are found to form a sequence that narrates "the Epic of Man and his Friends, of that brave company that has both angels and apes on its fringes." This Epic displays the "First Age of Magic" when man was "Lord of the World" and could fly, walk on water, move mountains, and, relevant to our focus on the non-human:

> *H*e could converse with both spirits and animals, as well as with the superior plants and trees, and the mountains. He traded repartee with the lightning, and he didn't do too badly in that exchange.

The Epic next depicted man's "fall" from this first magical age, and we hear language that recalls Quine's aesthetic preference for an ontology of desert landscapes. In this stage of the Epic

> *P*roud and benighted man was a castaway marooned on the Narrow Isthmus (the "Desert Island" of popular accounts). Desert Islands are dismal, dismal, dismal. But what if they become dismally romantic?

As the Epic unfolds it tells also of "good news" that man is now free to leave the ontological desert, the narrow isthmus. But this message is opposed by the "parathurouclasts" (the window-smashers), who adhere to a rival narrative, again in remarkably Quinean terms:

> *T*he desert-island-isthmus was the world, the only world there had ever been, the only world there could be allowed to be... Sure it was dismal, but certainly there was a strong and dismal romantic attachment to it. The Establishment had buried all its treasure on that desert island, and it could not go away and leave it.

As the story closes the Stained Glass Epic is destroyed, but then resurfaces to haunt those who reject it and call them to repentance.

Laffertian Thomism

For Lafferty, all these wide-angle sympathies we've been tracking in his writing are simply his unique and characteristically off-kilter exemplification of Thomistic theology.[1] As Chesterton noted in his *St Thomas Aquinas*: "If St. Thomas stands for one thing more than another, it is what may be called subordinate sovereignties or autonomies... We might even say he was always defending the independence of dependent things. He insisted that such a thing could have its own rights in its own region" (p. 29 in the 1943 Hodder and Stoughton edition). Aquinas, Chesterton duly notes, is motivated to this sort of "Materialism" through the doctrines of Creation, Incarnation, and Resurrection, where the material, the physical, is caught up into the divine – or the divine

---

1See Gregorio Montejo's essay in this volume for a more sophisticated explication of Lafferty as a Thomist regarding the philosophy of time.

comes down into the material. Rather than an escapist, world-hating, pie-in-the-sky theology (reductionist in the opposite direction of Quinean metaphysics), Lafferty's Catholicism motivates his writing with a rich focus on material things because material things were, first of all, made to be their own integral thing; and secondly, are imbued with divinity; and lastly, may rise up into a glorified state, into, that is, an even deeper solidity and robustness (see C. S. Lewis's *The Great Divorce* for a vivid picture of a glorified material state – though I have no idea if Lafferty ever read this particular book by Lewis, he does mention him alongside Kafka, Don Marquis, Aldous Huxley, and others as a "very good" author in his aforementioned essay "The Case of the Moth-Eaten Magician"). Chesterton, following Aquinas, corrects the tendency we might have when we learn that Lafferty is a Christian, which is that we might think him interested mainly in immaterial souls and getting them to an immaterial heaven and the like. This is not so because "a Christian *means* a man who believes that deity or sanctity has attached to matter or entered the world of the senses" (p. 31).

Because of this theologically driven commitment to the integrity of each created thing, Chesterton says "we may say broadly that St. Thomas comes down definitely on the side of Variety, as a thing that is real as well as Unity" (p. 30). So it is with Lafferty also. Chesterton evokes a similar resonance with Lafferty when he says Aquinas "was ready to take the lowest place; for the examination of the lowest things. He did not, like a modern specialist, study the worm as if it were the world; but he was willing to begin to study the reality of the world in the reality of the worm" (p. 70). (Interestingly, worms put in appearances in Lafferty's tales far more than the few times already cited above.)

This Thomistic view, where "the extremes of heaven and earth meet", is what makes Lafferty so very earthy and spiritual at once. Because of both its wide sweep and its love of discrete objects,

Chesterton also notes: "The Thomist movement in metaphysics, like the Franciscan movement in morals and manners, was an enlargement and a liberation" (p. 30), and it is clear that this is exactly how Lafferty sees his work. That is why he urges us out of the sterile desert and off of the narrow isthmus.

We can see from the copious and capacious lists in Lafferty's writing (and I have by no means cited all of them – the longest I have found so far is a delightfully erudite two or three pages worth of old objects in an old room in the 1974 story "And Read the Flesh Between the Lines") that Lafferty, like Aquinas, "was enormously interested in everything." He "was avid in his acceptance of Things; in his hunger and thirst for Things. It was his special spiritual thesis that there really are Things, and not only the Thing; that the Many existed as well as the One" (Chesterton, p. 108). And Lafferty echoes Aquinas not only in "his broad and virile appetite for the very vastness and variety of the universe" but also in his belief in the source of that variety, for when Aquinas, Chesterton tells us, looked

> Between the outstretched arms of the Crucified, those arms were truly opened wide, and opening most gloriously the gates of all the worlds; they were arms pointing to the east and to the west, to the ends of the earth and the very extremes of existence. They were truly spread out with a gesture of omnipotent generosity; the Creator himself offering Creation itself; with all its millionfold mystery of separate beings, and the triumphal chorus of the creatures. (page 108)

As for Aquinas, so for Lafferty. Indeed, we can see a very similar kind of portrait of a Cosmic Christ in one last witness from

Lafferty's writing in this article, yet another erudite list.

The Most Fulfilled, the Most Shatteringly Profound Image Ever

Lafferty's novelistic history *The Fall of Rome* (1971), opens with the "Prologue of the Picture", which returns to the theme of all the variety of things "adding up" to some Great Vision. The prologue begins: "Near the end of the fourth century, the Mosaic-of-the-Great-Picture came into its own." Lafferty informs us:

> *T*he great mosaics were made up of thousands of small cubes or tesserae imbedded in a matrix of plaster or cement or clay. The colored cubes formed intricate pictures, one picture merging into another: these smaller pictures, when seen from a distance and in the right aspect, would form one great picture. Most persons could see it clearly: some could not see it at all.

All the ingredients of Lafferty's artistry are given here: myriad pieces, embedding, matrix, intricacy, merging pictures, and smaller pictures forming one great picture (if you have eyes to see it).

Lafferty then provides another detail of this ancient art that reflects something crucial about his own: "The cubes were set into the matrix with an unevenness that was an art, so that the light off them shattered and gave a sheen and sparkle to the whole arrangement." Sure, Lafferty was a limited artist like anyone and his works can come across "uneven" simply for the reason that he, though a consummate craftsman and a genius, was not flawless. But a lot of that unevenness can be seen, on reflection and repeated reading, to be an intentional artistry of its own that gives his work a shattering "sheen and sparkle" overall. These bristling lists we have lingered over are an example of that, I think. They practically career off the page, and can seem to have little to do with the plot, but they are crucial to much of the effect that Lafferty achieves, especially as regards an object-opulence that coalesces into an encompassing vision of life. What could be more shining and shattering?

Now here it is, a last (comparatively brief and straightforward, yet very encompassing) list that "adds up":

> *T*he smaller pictures were of people, animals, actions, furniture and handicrafts, towns, fields, banquets, worships, labours and pleasures, buildings, ships, plows, soldiers, children, courtesans, sheep, and asses. They combined in the great picture (which not everyone could see), the face of Christ.

Lafferty goes on for another whole page and a bit more, making cascading lists of cities and nations and popes and generals and kings and mentioning that the picture is made up also of lords and ladies and Goths and "the translucent tesserae of the saints and martyrs like chips of lapis lazuli" and so on. And then he makes this utterly crucial conclusion, a development of the earlier statement about the face of Christ:

> *S*ometimes the picture of the passion and death of the Empire will be the face of the crucified Christ: but often there will emerge the most fulfilled, the most shatteringly profound image ever, the laughing Christ of Creophylus.

Andrew Ferguson has argued persuasively in his paper

"Lafferty and His World" that Lafferty's worldview is one rooted in "cosmic laughter". Thus it is no surprise to see the mosaic of Lafferty's encyclopedic erudition adding up not just to the face of Christ, but, at its fullest and most wondrous, the face of the Laughing Christ. (The actual statue of the laughing Christ, by the ancient sculptor Creophylus, reappears in the cast of characters that populate Lafferty's 1988 novel *East of Laughter*. I hope to touch on that in the next article.) All these delightful objects have their own integrity and Lafferty celebrates them without end. Yet he also sees them collaborating to build a salvific and all-encompassing vision, at times in travail, but ultimately joyous.

Lafferty knows, of course, that some of us just can't see it. And some would go so far as to forbid the seeing of it. As characters discuss in *Serpent's Egg*:

> "Well, what is our Rationale of Life? We are forbidden to have a Theology of Life (have you noticed how forbidding the Floating World has become?), but may we not at least have a Rationale of Life?"

> "I don't think so, Inneall," Lutin the Pythoness said. "The most we can hope for is a Mystique of Life." (p. 141)

One thinks of Thomas More's response to similar censoriousness in *Past Master* (1968): "I forbid the forbidding."

At any rate, Lafferty's wide and deep ontic gaze, inclusive though it is of (for example) the supernatural, is probably more inclusive of "natural" and material non-human phenomena and entities than you are likely to find in many other places. You may not agree with Lafferty's ontology. You may not think things exist that he thinks exist. You may populate the universe quite radically different than him. But read Lafferty, read tons of Lafferty, and see if he does not, at the very least, make you see much more of what you *do* think exists. See if he doesn't broaden your horizons even on your own terms, so that your ontic gaze is more sweeping and layered and rich – indeed, bristling and roiling! And maybe, just maybe, you will even gain some ontic humility, and grow in your sense of ontic humour, and even (who knows?) re-open the case files on a few sorts of being you thought couldn't be. Lafferty is nothing if he's not an eye-opener.

Envoy:

At the celebration of Lafferty's centenary, in our enthusiasm and hope for the flourishing of his works, we may be pardoned if we compare his mind to that that of the Catholic church's greatest theologian. Add in wheels of oddities and arcana to Chesterton's picture of Aquinas's mind painted below and that might be a glimpse of Lafferty's great mind as well, exemplifying what OOO theorists call the "bizarre bazaar" of an object-opulent universe. I don't know if any of Lafferty's avid admirers were in attendance at his deathbed (I doubt it), but if any of us had been, we might well have felt as Chesterton here imagines the monks surrounding Aquinas felt as he gave his final confession and breathed his final breaths (pp. 114-15):

> *T*hose men must have felt that, for that moment, the inside of the monastery was larger than the outside. It must have resembled the case of some mighty modern engine, shaking the ramshackle building in which it is for the moment enclosed. For truly that machine was made of the wheels of all the worlds; and revolved like that cosmos of concentric spheres

which, whatever its fate in the face of changing science, must always be something of a symbol for philosophy; the depth of the double and triple transparencies more mysterious than darkness; the sevenfold, the terrible crystal. In the world of that mind there was a wheel of angels, and a wheel of planets, and a wheel of plants or animals; but there was also a just and intelligible order of all earthly things, a sane authority and a self-respecting liberty, and a hundred questions in the complexity of ethics and economics. But there must have been a moment, when men knew that the thunderous mill of thought had stopped suddenly; and that after the shock of stillness that wheel would shake the world no more; that there was nothing now within that hollow house but a great hill of clay; and the confessor, who had been with him in the inner chamber, ran forth as if in fear, and whispered that his confession had been that of a child of five.

A deep-voiced man named Jack Edward Otis was a six foot seven, one-legged preacher from Florida. He liked to take off his wooden leg at the beach and wave his knee-stump at his embarrassed children (later to the delight of his grandchildren). His sonorous laughter could shake the fur off a dog. His small wife Ena, when they went out on Jack's boat, liked to drag her hand in the sea in hopes of collecting 'whale chips' to give to her grandchildren as souvenirs to take back to their land-locked Indianapolis home. (The grandchildren were delighted at this too.) In retirement old Jack and Ena lived in a little mobile home on a canal from which alligators occasionally emerged. (The grandchildren were duly warned to be aware of this and play safe.) The couple had one room full of Jack's World War II era model airplanes hanging from the ceiling and another room full of Ena's collected seashells (and one sun-bleached ox skull inside of which you could hear the cockroaches buzzing).

Otto Andreas Petersen was a five foot seven immigrant from Norway who was attached to a sequence of jobs and ladies, the latter including Viola, Jane, and Olive. Otto and Olive eventually settled on the northern west coast in Oregon. Daniel Eberg Petersen was the estranged child of Otto and Viola and this 'Danny' (as he was known then) grew up with the Wakemans in Arizona. Danny went by 'OJ' after recovering from alcoholism and taking up preaching himself. He then married a beautiful young flower child ten years his junior, Nolena Grace, the youngest of the five children of Jack and Ena Otis in Florida. OJ and Nolena moved to Indianapolis, Indiana and decided to name their second child after all three of the men in the foregoing account. That child now lives in Glasgow, Scotland and blogs about Lafferty at AntsOfGodAreQueerFish.blogspot.co.uk. He is also the author of the foregoing essay.

Illustration by Jack-Lewis Petersen
(instagram.com/sadpartytime)

Bellota was made for fun. It is a joke, a caricature, a burlesque. It is a planet with baggy pants and a putty nose. It is a midget world with floppy shoes and a bull-roarer voice. It was designed to keep the cosmos from taking itself too seriously. The law of levity here conspires against the law of gravity.

-R. A. Lafferty, "Snuffles" (1961)

AEVITERNITY: R.A. LAFFERTY'S THOMISTIC PHILOSOPHY OF TIME IN THE ARGO CYCLE

by Gregorio Montejo

*H*old everything right there! The hour grows early again, and there will never be a better place for some short notes on the nature of time and related things. The things related to time are aeon and eternity. . . .

There has always been a quantity of unreality leaking out of the future into the present. Then the unreality has to be negated, and the reality revived. The reconstructing of reality is what is being talked about when we talk about reconstructing the world.

R.A. Lafferty: *More Than Melchisedech: Argo* (Weston, Ontario: United Mythologies Press, 1992).[2]

The Chronic Argonauts

R.A. Lafferty built a vast cycle of fictional works around the voyages of the Argo—a vessel that shares its name, and in some

---

2N.B.: This edition of *More Than Melchisedech: Argo* was printed without page numbers, so all quotations from this particular text are given sans pagination.

sense identity, with the mythical ship upon which Jason and the Argonauts sailed in search of the legendary Golden Fleece, but in Lafferty's various fictions in which the Argo and its motley crew of mariners (including one named Finnegan, who in the past may have been not only Jason, but also Dionysius, Ulysses, as well as the Finn McCool of Celtic lore) are featured—among them the novels *Archipelago*, *The Devil Is Dead*, and the More Than Melchisedech trilogy (*Tales of Chicago*; *Tales of Midnight*; *Argo*) —the ship symbolically stands for more than this. As Lafferty explains, the Argo has voyaged numerous times during the unfolding of human history, at least fourteen times down the course of the ages. Yet each of these individual "trips aren't voyages, even if we may carelessly call them so. Each voyage is a cycle of trips or adventures, a dynasty of adventures. And a voyage is halted only by hiatus or mutation, or by one of the 'deaths' of the Ship. The Ship may be lost and found again several times on one of the voyages."

Moreover, the Argo is also a "dating clock, among very many other things," recording events for the past nine thousand years, and even future events that have not yet occurred, at least from the perspective of our present. "Most logs do not go into the future at all," the Argo's erstwhile captain during its fourteenth and perhaps final voyage explains, "so this is in the Argo's favor, however far it goes. But in this case, I think that — ah – I get the impression that that's all the farther the future goes. Or else the future moves into some other context about then." In addition, there are "several other ways in which the Argo acts as a dating clock." For example, if one "brings any artifact at all on board and touches it to the piece of talking oak that is built into the ship's wheel, that talking oak will call out the year of origin of the piece in whatever aeon or era it belongs, and in whatever annals of the era."

A *Topos* of Space-Time

How are we to understand the Argo and its particular relation to time? More broadly, what do these curious temporal features indicate about Lafferty's conception of time itself as he chronicles the Argo's spatio-temporal voyages? Perhaps the best way to begin to answer these questions is to look at Lafferty's notion of a temporal events themselves. In Lafferty's estimation, all time-bound occurrences are to be simultaneously mapped out in relation to both their chronometric and geo-spatial locations; in other words, in order to be grasped and understood as temporal phenomena, each discrete event must be situated within a fourfold space-time topology: "An event is like a box or other geometrical object . . . and it should be pretty much the same no matter which side it is viewed from." "Let us say," Lafferty continues, that "we look at it from the south side (that is the past), or from the east side (that is the present), or from the west side (that is an alternative present), or from the north side (that is the future). The event will look a little bit different from these various viewpoints, but not much. You must not reject one view of it when you come to another view. They are all equally parts of it."

Time, Time, Where Have You Gone?
The Future Isn't Quite What It Used To Be

Is it possible to locate this Laffertarian understanding of temporality within modern philosophical conceptions of time? Contemporary philosophers attempt to explicate the paradoxical nature of time by positing two fundamental modes by which one may describe the temporal ordering or relation among events. According to the first mode, Presentism, only things which are present now are taken to be actual or real. The past and the future are not presently actualized or real, thus if any statements about the past are true, then this is the case only because some event in the present moment makes this past event true. Presentists who deny the present reality of the past can be distinguished from advocates of Presentism who posit a special ontological status to events happening now, but who nevertheless ascribe a certain attenuated reality to past events, certainly inasmuch as the past, as a totality of already actualized events, grows over time into an ever larger block of space-time. The growth of time happens in the present, within that thin temporal slice designated as the "now" where space-time comes into being. Notwithstanding these distinctions, both groups of Presentists continue to claim that the future is not real.

By contrast, advocates of Eternalism deny not only the reality of the future, but refuse to endow either the present or the past with any exceptional ontological significance, for the particular importance that we assign to the present moment is purely subjective. Objectively speaking, there are no ontological differences between past, present, or future. The Eternalist view of time is usually associated with a four-dimensional view of the space-time manifold, wherein events are positioned in a coordinate system comprised of both spatial (length, width, height) and temporal dimensions. So whereas the Presentist theory of time posits a growing unitary block of space-time sliced into thin segments—or planes of simultaneous events—alongside an ever-growing segment of past actualizations, the four-dimensionalist Eternalist position would further adduce these events to be four-dimensional objects composed of a potentially infinite number of time-slices or spatio-temporal parts, which are only then subjectively identified as past, present, or future event, since the block itself makes no objective way of making such distinctions.

"Time Passages, There's Something Back Here That You Left Behind"

Lafferty certainly seems to position himself within a four-dimensional view of space-time, at least insofar as his temporal topology includes both spatial and chronometric elements in the descriptions of objects/events. Unlike proponents of Presentism, he ascribes a measure of ontological reality to the future (or perhaps we should say potential futurity), which as we have seen is recorded—at least partially—in the log of the Argo. However, unlike the Eternalists, he does seem to ascribe a privileged ontological status to the present, which unlike the past, can be changed: "We can change the present in the process of happening, by being a part of that happening. And often we can change the future which has not already happened. But not all our piety or wit will blot out any line of the past. Besides, we have already lived through the past, or died from it. Let us go on to other things." Indeed, if the future has an eschatological dimension insofar as it is the resolution of chronological time when all mundane events will reach their ultimate fruition, then Lafferty seems to hold for a kind of realized eschatology, wherein the future in some sense is already present in the now, and the present moment is suffused with and influenced by the not-yet of the future. "Forward into time or sideways in time," Biloxi Brannagan, another member of the Argo proclaims; since the Argo is moving at once "into the future or into the present." To which Melchisedech Duffey responds:

Every attempt to get the people to change the present to improve the future has been a dismal failure, though it would be the best way if it worked. But there is a very great amount of spill-back from the future into the present. Almost all of the worst effects of the present come from the future, and the future is

continually turning into the present. The future
is trial balloon country. Some of the balloons are
mighty evil, and if they are not shot down at
once they will drift into reality. Prescient types
see some of the things that are trying to
become, and we do what we can about them.
We are constantly moving out in front and
making changes in things before they happen.

Of Time and Timelessness

The key to understanding this flow of influence both forwards
and backwards between the present and the future is to be found in
Lafferty's conception on how the flow of temporal events relates to
eternity and to what he refers to as the Aeon. Aristotle defined
time as the "numbered of things" in the *Physics* (233b); in other
words, time is the enumeration of motion in a sequence of events
understood as a causal chain extending all the way back to a first
mover which sets the sequence in motion. This notion of time as
the measure of motion was adopted in the middle ages by Thomas
Aquinas and other Scholastics who noted that time and motion
were invariably experienced in relation to one another. That is to
say, temporal events succeed each other in a series of motions, and
each motion occurs in its own "now", since when one motion is
succeeded by a subsequent one, these two "nows" are perceived to
be before and after in between the middle term. Hence, in this
manner, temporal events are enumerated as before and after in
motion, not because time itself is in motion, for Thomas adapts
Aristotle's notion of temporality to conclude that time is "nothing
other than the number of motion according to before and after" (In
Sent. I, d.19, q.2, a.1: tempus est numerus motus secundum prius et
posterius).

And this is precisely the conceptualization of time that Lafferty propounds when he writes in *More Than Melchisedech: Argo* that "Time is the measure of the duration of material creatures and substances. It is the numbering of the successiveness of material change", for those things that "do not change do not have a beginning and end, and do not display successiveness." From this definition, one could infer that since there are many successive "nows", there must also be a multiplicity of times. After all, Lafferty notes, an "instant of time is imperfect, and anything that is imperfect may be added to." Suppose, he further considers, a person who only lives "every odd millisecond of an instant, or every third millisecond of it? He would still be living with successiveness and would still be living through imperfect instants. Then those instants could, in another successiveness, be added to. This would not be living that instant twice, though it would resemble it very closely." Nevertheless, Lafferty concludes his thought experiment with a firm no; this sort of thought experiment is mere sophistry, for "there is only one time." That is, there is only the reckoning of succession in the soul or mind of man. With Aristotle, Lafferty could thus rightly claim that time arose with the birth of humanity: "There would not be time unless there were soul, but only that of which time is an attribute." To be more precise, the objects of time—particular things engaged in their particular motions—existed prior to man, yet time itself did not, since there were no humans around to perceive and conceptualize it. Brute time then is merely the motions of the mind/soul in response to the material motions of things in the cosmos.

In stark contradistinction to time as the enumerations of before and after in the human psyche, Lafferty posits eternity, that which "lacks both beginning and end", and therefore "exists as a single instant lacking successiveness but having immeasurable depth." To put it another way, "eternity is perfect, and anything that is perfect cannot be added to"; needless to say, there "is only one eternity." Quoting Boethius, Lafferty adds that while the "flowing instant produces time," it is the "abiding instant" that produces eternity. This last point indicates that the central feature of eternity is not the fact that it does not begin or end in time, but rather that eternity's lack of temporal origin or finitude bespeaks the perfection of self-subsistent being. Lafferty reinforces this point with a long question from Aquinas: "Time and eternity clearly differ. But certain people make the difference consist of time having a beginning and an end whilst eternity has neither. Now this is an accidental and not an intrinsic difference... eternity is an instantaneous whole, whilst time is not; eternity measuring abiding existence and time measuring change."

Here, Lafferty recalls an "old school-boy argument that states that, since eternity does not have a beginning, then obviously it has not begun; and that the abiding existence is not yet." But rather than undermining the argument for the enduring existence of eternity, this reference to beginnings will be the basis for a much more cogent argument positing the notion of those things that begin and change as necessitating the existence of an eternal, unchanging source of motion that is not moved by anything beyond itself. As Aquinas observes in another context, all material objects are in motion—they come to be and pass away, they change—this is the very motion which makes our perception of time possible. Moreover, if something is in motion, then it must be caused to be in motion by something outside of itself; however, there can be no infinite regress of such moved movers. Therefore, at the beginning of this causal sequence of movement there must be a first unchanging Unmoved Mover and Uncaused Cause which causes itself to move and which in turn is the cause of all other things in motion. And this eternal, first, and necessary cause is what is generally acknowledged as God, for the "idea of eternity follows immutability, as the idea of time follows movement. Inasmuch as he is the first mover, God is supremely immutable, thus it supremely belongs to Him to be eternal. Nor is He eternal only; but He is His own eternity; whereas, no other being is its own duration, as no other is its own being" (ST I, q.10, a.2, sc.: ratio aeternitatis consequitur immutabilitatem, sicut ratio temporis consequitur motum, ut ex dictis patet. Unde, cum Deus sit maxime immutabilis, sibi maxime competit esse aeternum. Nec solum est aeternus, sed est sua aeternitas, cum tamen nulla alia res sit sua duratio, quia non est suum esse). Eternity then is God's own being, which is the "simultaneously-whole and perfect possession of interminable life" (ST I, q.10, a.1, ad.1: aeternitas est interminabilis vitae tota simul et perfecta possession).

The Metaxy of Time and Eternity

It is with these two notions of time and eternity explicated that we can now turn to Lafferty's crucial introduction of the concept of the Aeon. In Plato, aeon (alternatively, aiōn or eon) is the eternal, more often than not, as it is participated in by temporal creatures:

When the father creator saw the creature which he had made moving and living, the created image of the eternal (*aidios*) gods, he rejoiced, and in his joy determined to make the copy still more like the original; and as this was eternal (*aidios*), he sought to make the universe eternal, so far as might be. Now the nature of the ideal being was eternal (*aiōnios*: ἡ μὲν οὖν τοῦ ζῴου φύσις ἐτύγχανεν οὖσα αἰώνιος), but to bestow this attribute in its fullness upon a creature was impossible. Wherefore he resolved to have a moving image of eternity (*aiōnos*), and when he set in order the heaven, he made this image eternal (*aiōnios*) but moving according to number, while eternity (*aiōnos*) itself rests in unity; and this image we call time (chronos). For there were no days and nights and months and years before the heaven

> was created, but when he constructed the heaven he created them also. They are all parts of time, and the past and future are created species of time, which we unconsciously but wrongly transfer to the eternal (*aidios*) essence (*Timaeus*, 37c-e).

As the mediation of eternity to the temporal, the aiōn is particularly identified with metaxy (μεταξύ), that condition of in-betweenness that is a constituent characteristic of humanity, suspended as it is between two poles of existence: the infinite and the finite, the necessary and the contingent, the one and the many, and the eternal and the temporal. In Gnosticism, the mediatorial aeons bridge the seemingly unbridgeable gulf between the transcendent and the immanent; in effect successive emanations from God from eternity into the spatio-temporal world order. In Medieval Latin Scholasticism, especially Thomas Aquinas, the *aevum* or Aeon is the particular ontological modality of spiritual entities, such as angelic beings, or those material creatures who have gained access to the beatific vision of the immutable and eternal divine essence: It is the halfway house between the eternity of God's *esse* and the temporal existence of purely material beings. Succinctly categorized, just as time has a beginning and an end as measured by the motions of before and after, and eternity is a perfect existence with neither beginning nor end, then aeviternity —life in the *aevum*—has a beginning in time but no ending (ST I, q.10, a.5, sc.: dicentes quod aeternitas principio et fine caret; aevum habet principium, sed non finem; tempus autem habet principium et finem).

This is what Lafferty has in mind when he writes that the "Aeon is the measure of the duration of non-material creatures or substances, as time is that of material creatures or substances." Since aeviternity partakes of God's divine eternity, it would seem incompatible with any kind of change whatsoever, which, as we have seen, is measured by notions of before and after. Lafferty begins to answer this conundrum by quoting Aquinas to the effect that "although the aeon is instantaneously whole, it differs from eternity in being able to exist with before and after" (ST I, q.10, a.5, ad.2: aevum est totum simul, non tamen est aeternitas, quia compatitur secum prius et posterius). For Thomas, this openness within the *aevum* to some aspects of change is most readily apparent in angelic beings who—as separate substance—have eternal life and "unchangeable being as regards their nature," but who also possess "changeableness as regards choice"; as well as changeableness of "intelligence, of affections and of places in their own degree." Therefore these beings are measured by aeviternity "which is a mean between eternity and time" (ST I, q.10, a.5, c.: Et similiter patet de Angelis, quod habent esse intransmutabile cum transmutabilitate secundum electionem, quantum ad eorum naturam pertinet; et cum transmutabilitate intelligentiarum et affectionum, et locorum suo modo. Et ideo huiusmodi mensurantur aevo, quod est medium inter aeternitatem et tempus). This is quite different from "being that is measured by eternity", which is not changeable, nor "annexed to change." Hence, we can characterize time as having a before and an after, while aeviternity in itself has no before or after, however, this notion can "be annexed to it" (Ibid: Sic ergo tempus habet prius et posterius, aevum autem non habet in se prius et posterius, sed ei coniungi possunt).

Aeviternal Manifolds

As members of that metaxological order of creation which straddles both the material and the spiritual realms, humans for Lafferty are paradigmatically aeviternal, with one foot in the temporal flux of measured motion, and the other in the unchanging duration of God's eternal esse. Privileging Origen's interpretation of the Aeon, according to which there are multiple aeviternal manifolds—a position that Thomas himself considers, seems to find disturbing, and ultimately rejects, since he envisions a unitary aeviternity hierarchically ordered to the eternity of an immutable God (Cf. ST I, q.10, a.6, c.)—Lafferty contends that there is "one aeon for every immaterial individual and for every immaterial relationship." Moreover, some "aeons apply only to the non-material aspects of individuals and relationships", and a person "who is partly material and partly immaterial will be sometimes in time and sometimes in aeon. There are more aeons than one." Can an aeviternal chrononaut anticipate the way the future will unfold in the present and attempt to change it?

*O*ne can try. There is a thin leading edge between the devouring present and the waiting future. What happens if one is too eager and crosses this leading edge? The world ends, for that person, for that while... If this thin line is crossed, then one is out in the narrow interval of unreality. It's a chancy though flexible place there... Melchisedech Duffey and his history had come up to the absolute present time, and then had gone a thumb's width beyond that, Duffey and his nimbus had gone into the future then? No, they had gone into the shattering state of contingency. It was a fracturing of reality. And it was a fracturing of Melchisedech Duffey.

The fracturing of Melchisedech Duffey can then perhaps be construed most pertinently as a *transitus*, not just an uncertain passage between the "devouring present" and the "waiting future," but a treacherous crossing betwixt the ceaseless flow of chronometric motion and the "annexed" spiritual movements at play in the aeonic arena. As Lafferty dramatically illustrates in the course of the Argo Cycle, it is in this "narrow interval" of unreality where both futurity and the "now" are eschatologically present to each other, and thus open to an especially radical form of contingency, that we encounter the trans-temporal "before" and "after" of men who are situated in the fourfold temporal flux, yet are nevertheless capable of gazing directly at the unchanging essence of God, and so are called to make those fateful choices whose effects are ultimately measured not in days, or years or even centuries, but in terms of aeviternity, that perilous meeting place between eternity and time.

> *D*uffey had been into the future before, spottily, off and on, for seven years once. And he had returned several times to those same seven years. And yet it was not strictly speaking into the future. It was a mixture of future and past and present. It was an interval or series of intervals removed out of time and held apart. The intervals of Seven Years did not necessarily count in regular time, which is why they could sometimes be revisited. They did not fracture reality. They stood on the far side of reality.

⟞⟡⟝

Gregorio Montejo (http://www.bc.edu/schools/cas/theology/faculty/gmontejo.html) is a professor of Historical Theology at Boston College. His research interests include Thomas Aquinas, Medieval Theology, Christology, Trinitarian Theology, and Pneumatology. Gregorio is a member of the Catholic Theological Society of America, the Society of Biblical Literature, the North American Patristics Society, etc.

SOME NOTES ON PLAY, TIME AND CATHOLIC SOCIAL TEACHING IN R.A. LAFFERTY

by John Ellison

In two of Lafferty's short stories we find characters who have experienced revelatory moments of beauty and happiness but who now struggle to locate the sites where these events occurred. In "Maybe Jones and the City" we are told that:

> *O*nce Maybe Jones had found the Perfect Place. He had left it, and he was never able to find it again... He didn't know where the place was, nor its name nor its direction, nor any way to identify it. He looked for it forever and he and it became legends. (pp. 181-183 in *Does anyone else have something further to add?*, Dobson edition, 1979)

In "Configuration of the North Shore" the patient Miller describes his wish "To visit the Northern Shore, and to make the visit stick", while admitting that he had searched for twenty five years without finding its location. Later in this story the central search-motif switches to the analyst Rousse who sees something:

> [...] *t*hat nobody else had ever seen before. He looked at the shape of the new sky that is always above the world and is not above the abyss. From the configuration of the sky he read the Configuration of the Northern Shore.

He gasped with unbelief. Then the dream
broke... (p. 180 in *Lafferty in Orbit*, Broken
Mirrors edition, 1991)

There is a sense that these stories are emblematic of how the
reader and critic deals with the writings of Lafferty. There are
common accounts of feelings of wonder and enchantment from
fans of Lafferty. Yet alongside this there is a kind of implicit
understanding that the processes whereby the stories actually work
on the reader are quite elusive. We often can't go back into the first
evocations and ambience felt when reading a particular Lafferty
story. It is as if each encounter with a Lafferty tale has an
elemental aspect of dream and myth which won't simply line up
with the words on the page. It is likely, then, that, like Maybe
Jones and Rousse and Miller, we are searchers after evasive
patterns and lost memories. If we grant this, are there relevant
strategies that can be adopted?

One manner of proceeding may be to try and sneak up on
certain themes in Lafferty instead of confronting his works head-
on with ready-made explanatory models. I have always liked the
blocks of quotes that break up certain of Lafferty's short stories
and novels. It may be appropriate to start to use this technique to
open up ideas in Lafferty.

In his essay "Playfulness: A Meditation", published in *The
Maynooth Review* in June 1976, Noel Dermot O' Donoghue states:

If one listens with the ear of the spirit one can
hear the music of fountains, the voice of God as
the sound of many waters. And something deep
in us responds to this. Through it we discover
that dimension, for many the most hidden of all,
the dimension of playfulness...The function of

playfulness is to place all finite reality in question, and so it is, to use Peter Berger's term, a signal of transcendence, an indication of a larger world. So it is that it decompresses, releases, provides space and scope. At its highest it is the stirring of spirit as untrammelled and infinite disengaging itself from the seemingly inescapable iron grips of the finite temporal [...] (p. 56)

This contrast between the serious world of fate and the playful world of ordinary experience is shown in Lafferty's short story, "Or Little Ducks Each Day". Jim Snapjudge is a Prejudicial Analyst who predicts human behaviour using information from the external features and mannerisms of a person. Based on the briefest of encounters Snapjudge determines that Godfrey Halskragen will be shot and killed later that day. Yet from the moment of this judgment we are shown how the absolute aspect of his verdict begins to unravel:

*B*ut then Snapjudge did a thing that he did very seldom. He looked back. And the young man who had passed him also looked back at the same instant, and their looks met. Their thoughts crossed like two rapiers made out of swift sunlight.

"Could I not be different from my template?" the thought of the young man laughed back at Snapjudge. "Have I to die tonight just because my pattern says 'die'? May I not escape?" And the young man winked crookedly. (p. 167 in *Iron Tears*, Edgewood Press edition, 1992.)

There is scope for freedom and laughter in the ending of the story as Godfrey and his companions evade the fate that Snapjudge saw as a certain reality.

We can argue, then, that there are important philosophical issues that arise from a consideration of this story. Yet it is notable how Lafferty plays with the reader so that they also encounter discourses quite at odds with the logical explanatory models typically found in science fiction. We find George defining the situation to Snapjudge:

> *I* also know that fate can be subverted in a few neighbourhoods of this world. As to Rhineland here, this is the case: Originally God had jurisdiction over Ohio and the Devil had jurisdiction over Kentucky; and Rhineland was then a part of Kentucky. Then the course of the river changed on one stormy night and Rhineland ended up on the Ohio side. Neither God nor the Devil ever laid claim to Rhineland in its new situation though, and fate has had a very insecure time here with no higher jurisprudence to appeal to. I imagine that a similar account can be given of most of the other unruly sections of other towns. (ibid, p186)

We might extract the phrase "the other unruly sections" from the above quote and use it as a thematic heading for all those unique contexts in Lafferty's fiction. Stories like "One at a Time" and "Maybe Jones and the City" fit obviously into this kind of category. Yet there is always that sense in Lafferty that he does examine ideas from every possible angle and that seemingly quite different stories may be addressing the same issue. At one level, the story "The Hand with One Hundred Fingers" functions as a quite bleak dystopian vision of a "liberal totalitarian" society in which all people are made to conform to the projected consensus. Even the narrative discourse is made to support this consensus, adding to the claustrophobic effect of the story:

> *S*o those Person-Projectors did a job on Conchita and she became repulsive at once. *Became* repulsive? She had always been repulsive, of course. (p. 125 in *Lafferty in Orbit*, Broken Mirrors edition, 1991.)

The style and form of this and other stories dealing with control and manipulation such as "About a Secret Crocodile" and "Tom O'Shanty's Aura" are quite different from "One at a Time" and "Maybe Jones and the City". Yet we may still argue that underlying themes such as freedom and determinism are always being addressed in his work. Lafferty affirms the local over the global, the individual over the collective, fun and laughter over unthinking conformity.

The following passage in *Fourth Mansions* offers a kind of anticipatory insight to the rise of globalisation in the decades after the book was written:

> " *W*e come to apex, and it is in no way elevated or outstanding; we come to perfection, and to perfect means to finish; we come to climax, and it is beautifully flat and undistinguished. We have completed the world. Behold it!"

> And in some manner Michael Fountain *was* holding a large, fine, precious, crystal bowl, the Golden Glass Bowl, in his two hands. It was

pretty. It was almost substantial.

"This is the world," Michael intoned in a self-induced trance. "This is our lives, this is our final achievement. Worry not that it is small: it is the largest world ever, if we will not allow a larger one..." (p. 202, *Fourth Mansions*, Star Book edition 1977.)

Globalization has resulted in a smoothing over of cultural surfaces and a flattening of the distinctive things that serve to make existence human and alive. I would like to offer some quotes to support this belief from a seemingly unlikely source, an article which explores contemporary working practices for lawyers through the lens of Catholic theology.

*I*n the world of billable hours, then, time's value is purely instrumental; it is a commodity with an identifiable price; it is fungible not unique; and it is often experienced by those who live within its purview as an endless colorless extension. These four features of time in the world of billable hours are not distinct, but build upon and reinforce each other. The fact that time is fungible makes it easier to assign it a market value. Its status as a commodity reinforces the impression that its purpose is instrumentally to achieve the pre-existing goals of law firms and clients. Precisely because time is the medium through which personal and social existence take shape, the way in which it is understood can have substantial implications for the lives of both individuals and communities [...] the world of billable hours perceives time as an

endless extension, with project after project
extending into the horizon of the years ahead;
it does not encourage the inhabitants of that
world to step back a moment, to ponder their
lives as a whole, and to articulate a narrative
that unifies and gives purpose to the discrete
moments of their lives. (M. Cathleen Kaveny,
"Living the Fullness of Ordinary Time: A
Theological Critique of the Instrumentalisation
of Time in Professional Life", in *Communio:
International Catholic Review*, Winter 2001, pp.
789-90)

Later in the essay the writer continues:

*F*rom a Catholic Christian world view, time is
intrinsically rather than instrumentally valuable;
it is not a commodity but a mystery; its
moments are not fungible, but in significant
ways unique; it is not an endless colorless
present but a spiral punctuated by moments of
decision. Finally, viewed in proper theological
and liturgical perspective, time does not lead
to fragmentation and isolation, but calls for
personal integration and the nurturing of
community. (Ibid, pp. 809-10)

These comments can provide a useful entry-point for an
analysis of a writer who constantly played with the idea of time,
offering versions of slowed-up, speeded-up and changeable time
throughout his stories. Instead of the enclosed nature of the
consciousness of time within secular materialism, Lafferty gives us
open-ended realities full of life and exuberance.

What I would also like to draw from these considerations of the nature of time is the way we can build a picture of Lafferty which places him at the centre of contemporary political and cultural debates. Like Chesterton he was an advocate of that category of Catholic thought which is known as Catholic Social Teaching. Unlike Chesterton, Lafferty was alive to see and record from the 1960s onwards the increase of those tendencies that would undermine the ideals of solidarity, family life and subsidiarity that constitute Catholic Social Teaching. He pointed to the rise of the ideology of consensus, the use of media as a focus for hatred and scapegoating, and the cult of narcissistic self-affirmation.

The following passage from *The Flame is Green* refers to some of the pioneers of Catholic Social Thought from the 19th century.

> "*I* myself would join the Green Revolution—were it in existence to be joined. But the Green is no more than a hope only, a thin hope, and it breaks away into sea-green, eel-green, monster-green. The thing about it, Dana, is that it hasn't been formulated yet, and it may never be."
>
> "Not formulated at all, Brume?" Dana asked.
>
> "Only in scraps, by outlandish and contradictory people. Cobbett and Cobden in England, Ozanam and Buchez and Blaye and Cheve in France, August Olt in Alsace, the young Archbishop of Damiata who is named Vincent Pecci, and—"
>
> (p. 52, *The Flame is Green*, Corroboree Press edition, 1985.)

The tentative quality of this passage is useful. I am obviously wary of constructing any absolute verdict on a "political Lafferty" and so my argument is also, as it were, "not formulated". Yet Vincent Pecci went on to become Pope Leo XIII and wrote the foundational text of Catholic Social Teaching, the encyclical *Rerum Novarum*. And many governments in Europe now see Catholic Social Teaching as a major intellectual force and a necessary element to be incorporated within policy-making to counter the atomising effects of secular liberalism.

I would like to end by a re-consideration of the kind of "extreme play" that is portrayed in certain Lafferty stories. In "Among the Hairy Earthmen" and *The Three Armageddons of Enniscorthy Sweeny* history is shown functioning through various unexpected modalities. It appears that history with all its violence, war and destruction may be described in terms of a children's game or a set of unfolding dramas. These sets of visions do seem to strike some intuitive chord. We recognise that a kind of surreal madness enacted at various historical levels may be coming from beings or entities who are quite demonic in their aspect. What is significant, though, is the way this takes place through agencies connected with power and collective action. Is it possible to set Lafferty's ideas apart from similar writers whose use of the blood and violence of history may just be part of an aesthetic of the absurd and the nihilistic?

I believe Lafferty is different in that he constantly returns to the personal, the ordinary, the matter-of-fact and the ironic. He locates the true ground of experience in this area. A final quote from O' Donoghue's article is supportive of the kind of vision of play which can characterise the Catholic imagination of a writer like Lafferty.

What I am suggesting is that those who see a

malevolent or heartless playfulness behind the world are not leaving enough room for the deeper, further reaches of the Divine hiddenness. So far is the divine from the spirit of mockery and from the cruelty of the cat and mouse situation that it shatters this playfulness through a larger irony. It is the mouse that carries the divine likeness and significance (for thus his enemies played with the Perfect Man), as the lamb does, as he goes to be killed. We do not easily see that there may be a divine significance in little things even in the hen with her chicks under her wings. We find such things ridiculous, only because we are too serious, and are ridiculous in our seriousness. Within the immensity of the divine hiddenness each little thing has its place, each least event. For the divine joy, the divine spontaneity encloses it all and supports each least particle of it. (p. 62, "Playfulness: A Meditation," Noel Dermot O'Donoghue, in *The Maynooth Review*, June 1976.)

John Ellison lives in England. At an early age, he selected Lafferty as a favorite author after discovering his short stories in SF magazines and anthologies in the late 1960s. John writes that at this time, Catholicism informs most of his choices in life—

indeed he has shifted between the quite different milieu of Damon Runyon (he used to be a manager of betting shops) and Dorothy Day (he now works in the charity and voluntary sector).

John is a frequent commenter on Andrew Ferguson's Tumblr, "Continued on Next Rock." He has had one other essay on Lafferty published in Dan Knight's fanzine, Boomer Flats Gazette.

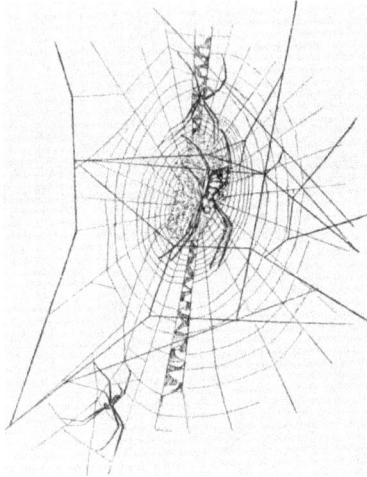

O GOLDEN, O SILKEN, O MOTHER-LOVING WORLD!

an original story by Daniel Otto Jack Petersen

Note: the following tale trepidatiously (foolhardily!) picks up where Lafferty's story, 'Once On Aranea' (collected in *Strange Doings*, 1972), left off. It should, however, be reasonably understandable whether or not one has read Lafferty's story.

\#

Emperor Scarble flung back his golden robes. The robes were voluminous and when he had them drawn about him they appeared to adorn a very ample form. But in moments such as now, when he flung them back with a flourish, it was seen that his frame was lean and wiry, still the frame of the trained and trim stellar explorer he had once been. Before his transformation. Before the whole Earth's transformation in the event known (by imperial decree) as the Golden Transcendence. The robes hung behind Scarble now in a royal train, and the source of the seeming bulk was revealed in all its dodecapodal glory.

He held his arms above his head in the Fingerling Salute, a gesture toward his millions of Earth children, those he indulged with infinitely patient Mother-Love, the same that had been shown to him by the mother-loving "spiders" of Aranea. He held his next pair of arms and the pair below them, and the pair below those, and, yes, the pair of arms below those, out to his sides in welcoming arachnidic greeting to his Earth cousins, the hundreds of millions of Original Spiders. These were those who had lent their name to their greaters. Their greaters were the super-terrestrial species of whom Scarble had been revealed to be the promised Messiah on that fortuitous expedition to Aranea, the Spider Asteroid of the planet-sized asteroids of the Cercyon Belt. It was an ordeal from which his peers thought he had emerged quite harmlessly mad, but it was proved they were the mad ones for not seeing the change that was on their cosmic doorstep. Emperor Scarble brought the fists of the lowest pair of arms back to his waist so that this pair of arms was akimbo, and he planted his legs (the twelfth pair of limbs on his glorified body) slightly apart in an unmistakable stance of command.

The Golden Emperor! The Mother-Loving Spider King! Lord of the Fingerlings and Master of the Fingerling's Best Friend (the Food-in-the-End)! Prefect Extraordinary to the Aranea Spiders of the Dispersal! Proconsul to the Spiders of Earth! Emperor of the Dodecapod Spiders of Aranea!

It had been said of Scarble, even before his transformation, that he looked like a spidery figure with his wiry, hairy limbs and small body. Now he was spider indeed.

He jutted his chin to his true subjects, the True Adults, the Spiders of Aranea (*Arachne Dodecapode Scarble* in the now outmoded "scientific" language). The Emperor need give no salute to the Other True Adults, his fellow transformed humans, the New Spiders of Earth, who stood guard at the circumference of this great gathering.

Stood guard? There was, of course, no need for security in this blessed Age of Security. But the humans had a long history of rebellions and uprisings, something the Araneans were not familiar with in the native ecology of their home world. So even these transformed ones, though now complete, could not entirely forget that race memory, and thus the vestigial "guards" of this gathering wielded in their five pairs of hands bolo knives, swords, glocks and pistols, spinning pairs of nunchaku, snicking switchblades, swishing machetes and a variety of other handheld weapons. The Aranean spiders were themselves consummate engineers (Emperor Scarble had witnessed firsthand the engineering wonders of their home world) and thus could have engineered far more precise and effective weapons than these crude cudgels the New Spiders brandished. There was, however, no need for such when their soporific-and-euphoria spider bites induced pleasant calm in all who were bitten, and their silken webs held the world close and safe in mother-love.

(Yes, there was that first bloody episode where machines of warfare were indeed needed, but that was forgiven and forgotten. Indeed, stranger resistances were told of. There was a story that Scarble himself had proposed marriage to one of the children, even before her transformation, but that she had spurned him, even in his glorified state, with one withering look. But the children were wayward and weird before their glorification and their perverse recalcitrance deserved only indulgent mother-love.)

There was no need for it, but the True Adults and their Emperor nevertheless indulged this residual weapon-wielding habit of the Other True Adults, the transformed humans, the New Spiders. Furthermore, they indulged (that is, swiftly and thoroughly suppressed in both the physical and psychological sense) the continual uprisings, really just scuffles, that still happened sometimes among the remaining "children" of the humans, the Fingerlings, who had not yet received their blessed transformation.

This massive ring of armed New Spiders was not seen by most, being too far to the perimeter of the mile-wide circle, and anyway they required no greeting from the Emperor. Their joy and allegiance were absolute. They lived to serve. They were, of course, only a small sampling of the millions more New Spiders who performed other tasks elsewhere in this land and across the planet.

(The number of the New Spiders should have been in the billions, but the majority of unglorified humans had died on the Night of the Hatching, the Dawn of the Golden Transcendence. For this majority, the Aranean spider bites had inexplicably induced rapid decay and dissolution rather than transformation, almost as if the people were deathly allergic to the golden serum. Then there was also the strange level of physical resistance they had put up, which the Araneans could only overcome by means of fatal bloodshed. Both circumstances had come as a surprise that the Aranean Spiders and their Emperor had nevertheless indulged —that is, expunged from memory—with patient mother-love.)

To the so-called Best Friends of the Fingerlings (as the people had come to be known in biological echo to a subservient species on Aranea), to the "dogs" in the old vulgar term, the Emperor also gave no greeting or acknowledgement. One doesn't greet the food one provides for one's children. For the dogs' part, they could only whimper a restrained affection if they dared. The beasts were belovedly stupid to the end.

Emperor Scarble stood thus, ten arms aloft, with his back to the sea, on the cliff edge of a long, reaching emerald outcrop on the middle East Coast of the United States of Arachnea. A natural plain stretched inland from this particular outcrop and here the assembly was taking place. The waves surged and broke behind the emperor from time to time, sending up a fine crackling spray that was made aureate by the morning sun. The reaching outcrop was the middle and longest Finger of the semi-natural formation known as the Twelve Fingers of Green-and-Gold Love. Seven of the outcrops had already existed at that location in the old USA when the spiders landed en masse on the Night of the Great Hatching. (Stay with us, those landing, incoming, arriving entities were the mother-loving spiders of Aranea, the True Adults, not the terrestrial arachnids, the Original Spiders.) Five more Fingers of land had been blasted and excavated and shaped in this new USA to complete the formation which had already been more than halfway to its fulfilment.

All other half-formed aspects of Earth had similarly now reached engineered fulfilment in the Golden Reign. The trillions of lines of the Golden Silk lay across all, wrapping the planet in silkiest steel, the mother-love. As littoral creatures, the Araneans dwelt by bodies of water and had engineered vast networks of pools and lakes and ponds all across the continents. There were a number of such pools in the midst of this gathering of the people, the children, that had been ritually prepared, and from which the children were soon to drink and take their first step in becoming full adults of the interplanetary Nation of Spiders.

"My children," intoned the emperor in golden, silken tones. (Scarble the spaceman hadn't talked like that before had he? No, he was transformed in voice and oratory as in all else.) "I address you first this Programmed Fools' Day, this Happy Hallowed Feast Day of Carnival Contrivance. Only this grotesque topsy-turvy day of the year do I speak to you, my wild and wayward children, before I speak to my true subjects, my spider army, your rightful dodecapod overlords. And yea, on this carnival day I will presently even deign to speak to your curs, your food-friends, and —impropriety of improprieties!—I will allow them to speak to me in return."

If one looked closely at the people, the children, one might notice a clenching of jaws and cording of arms at this imperial pronouncement, or a lowering of eyes, not in reverence, but in some kind of flustered embarrassment or shame. But the dogs licked their slack lips and tried not to utter hoarse moans, awaiting permission to really speak.

The children, the untransformed people of this assembly, were The Last Million whose number was at last fulfilled and who were gathered now for carnival on the eve of their long delayed transformation. They were the last of the strange resistance that had persisted (and was now forgotten) this past year. Their corralled number had actually exceeded a million by a sloppy few hundred, but the Araneans had neatly trimmed that fat (mostly the youngest and oldest of the untransformed people, for optimum efficiency) to make this an assembly of numerical exactness. The Last Million were arranged in the centre, each with a dog at his or her side. Around them in far greater number were their twelve-legged Aranean spider lords, rigid with attention and respect for their great and long-promised emperor, the one who they themselves had mother-loved into his present mode of being, back on their home world when he was but an unsuspecting explorer.

And flitting in and out of the whole were the Original Spiders, the arachnids of Earth, seeming bland in comparison to the many-jointed poise of their extra-terrestrial superiors. Where the people, the children, had once recoiled at the presence of the arachnids and sought to boot-stomp and book-smash them, they now gladly tolerated the presence of these old familiar eight-leggers, a welcome reminder that the world had not always been ruled by the twelve-leggers.

The Original Spiders had migrated to the gathering from all over the nation. *Bland in comparison?* How could such skin-crawling array ever seem bland? Oh, we suppose golden perfection could make it seem so. There were wolf spiders, grass spiders, black and yellow garden spiders, banded garden spiders, the hacklemesh weaver wove in and out in abundance, the cross orbweaver too, longlegged sac spiders, broad-faced sac spiders, dark fishing spiders, six-spotted fishing spiders, spotted orbweavers, barn funnel weavers, those wandering hunters the ant mimic spiders, giant house spiders, southern house spiders, eastern parson spiders, Carolina wolf spiders, woodlouse hunters, shabby and free-roaming hobo spiders, brown widows and black widows and false black widows, the Texas recluse and brown recluse were shy but present, gray wall jumpers, whitebanded crab spiders, giant crab spiders, goldenrod crab spiders, green lynx spiders, even common house spiders came out of their houses, and longbodied cellar spiders turned up, bold jumpers, tan jumping spiders, nursery web spiders, mouse spiders, those rude spitting spiders, and that unique little orbweaver, the arrowshaped microthena, shot about among the throng. Oh and there were many, many more. They were pretty interesting by Earth standards, we guess, but let us turn to more golden matters.

Emperor Scarble's many-limbed greeting and commanding stance were projected to the mile-wide assembly in twenty-feet high eidolons, at spaced intervals, in a large-scale controlled fractal pattern worked out by the mother-loving spiders, the Aranean master engineers. Thus, on the ground, all his children could see his majesty, and, from above, the locations of the eidolons formed the points of a mile-wide snowflake pattern, the Aranean symbol of silken sleep.

The emperor smiled upon the assembly below him, smiled oh so benevolently. There was gold in that smile, the good stuff that you could really hammer into.

Then he spoke: "Speak!"

And a million dogs set up a tidal wave of baying and barking. Indeed, the ocean waves periodically beating at Emperor Scarble's back were beaten back a little before the sonic wall of canine enthusiasm.

A million dogs? Yes, and maybe one or two more, enough to feed each Fingerling through his or her chrysalis stage, and in an array to match the spidery diversity. There were mastiffs, malamutes, hounds, huskies, terriers, spaniels, cockers, cattle dogs, bulldogs, shepherds, sheepdogs, sleddogs, seal dogs, deerhounds, elkhounds, pointers, pinschers, pugs, poodles, beagles, collies, bergers, berners, setters, schnauzers, retrievers, and more. And of every specification: Black Russian, Black Norwegian, Blackmouth, Afghan, Scottish, Russell, Russo-European, Pyrenean, Mexican Hairless, Himalayan, Hokkaido, Finnish, English, American English, Chinese, Chien-gris, Blanc et Noir, Blanc et Orange, Redbone, Billy, Basque, Mountain, Water, Farm, Fighting, Duck-Tolling, and so on.

Many of the people, the children, were paired off rather symmetrically with their dogs. There was a hefty mastiff of a man with a mastiff at his side, a scrappy bulldog of a fellow with a bulldog. There was a husky woman with a happy husky at her side. She looked like she could lift just about any of the men there onto her amorous shoulders and show him a good time (by the old ungolden idea of a good time). There was a smooth operator of a man, lean and leaning, with a wolfy-looking Tamaskan dog. Each dog was an appropriate meal for its person during metamorphosis. But there were apparent incongruities too. A compact and hard bitten Arab had a graceful greyhound at his side. Yet you could see the greyhound in his eyes if you looked closely. A very obese woman had two shih tzus snapping raptly at her heels. (It would take at least two to sustain her through chrysalis.) Yet her eyes also were each a snapping shih tzu.

There was an elderly man shaped like a great shambling pear. He had overlong hoar-frosted arms at the sides of his great clownish belly and two wispy Moses-horns of hair at the sides of his bald pate. He had in his long life been called a goblin, troll, ogre, gnome, and leprechaun. The old man had a faded lanyard around his neck from some bygone convention. It read: *G. I. O'Flaherty.* He had written with now faded marker above the faded print the names the initials stood for: *Gabriel Isidore.* He stood with a frisky Irish red and white setter. You couldn't see much of the man's eyes behind his grimed thick-lensed glasses, but you could see the Irish setter in the ghost of a grin at one corner of the old man's mouth, the same almost-curve seen in the dog's tail. One sensed that both the grin and the curve of the tail might wag into full being on a moment's notice.

This was the massive crowd in which the dogs had set up their gladsome baying. The Original Spiders, the arachnids of Earth, jumped anywhere from two to ten feet high all over the huge clearing, giving the impression of a network of in-ground sprinklers suddenly spraying into action, or of a ground-covering of sleeping crickets suddenly springing awake and a-leaping. The two actions, the barking and jumping, combined into some genuine comedy. It happened by the thousands in cascading pockets all across the assembly, a reversed staccato of un-noise. A dog would be cut short mid-bark as a terror-hopping spider would suddenly land in its mouth and be swallowed entire in a bewildered gulp. If the dog got to barking again, it was hoarse and spidery and the fun had gone out of it. Many of the people, those now called the children, who seemed otherwise grim of humor, could not refrain from a grin or chuckle at this, the kind of chuckling that is restrained for the sake of the feelings of the one you're laughing at, for they had no desire to shame their friends, the dogs, even at their slapstickery. The people felt their canine friends were being shamed enough and too much already in the new ecology. Any fun-loving humour between them should be kept private the people felt.

As Emperor Scarble, and all transformed humans, knew from experience, the dogs were to be putrefied and cocooned with their masters for their masters' sustenance while transforming. This was the way of transcendence. If the dogs (their diminutive biological equivalent on Aranea were called scutters) had any misgivings about this arrangement, it was not voiced. The people's misgivings were easier to read, however, even without voice.

The fractal-spaced eidolons of the Emperor spoke in perfect unison again:

"Peace!"

And the dogs choked themselves off even more thoroughly than if they had swallowed spiders, not so much as a whine now heard among the million of them.

"Carnival, carnival, oh my children and subjects and cousins, is it not grotesque?" Emperor Scarble cried.

This was giggling Aranean humor, thin and spiderlike, not the gross stuff that formerly passed for humor on Earth. Some said Scarble had possessed the spiderlike humor in some modicum even before transformed.

The spider lords, the True Adults and true subjects, minced their four fore-legs once in an audible clicking of assent to the Emperor's carnival cry. The children, the people, on the other hand, were loud with stony silence. The Original Spiders, the arachnids, had calmed themselves to mere crawling about again. The outer ring of the Other True Adults, the transformed humans, the New Spiders, continued lovingly caressing their weapons.

"And now that our carnival is over, I, Emperor of the Dodecapod Spiders of Aranea, address my true subjects, and command them to sing their mother-loving songs as only they can sing."

And the Aranean spiders set up their golden, silken song in a billion-thronged singing. They wove layer upon layer of complex and dreamy melodies around the people and their friends, the dogs. The ears on both pricked at the lovely, eye-heavying music. They sought to look nervously from side to side. But already they were held in place by the web of song alone, even before the fresh, fine silks began falling like a warm and comforting snow from the sky onto them as the Aranean spiders shot out their nearly invisible ribbons of silk in tandem with their now flossy-voiced singing.

There was a false note somewhere.

Impossible. This was the flawless singing of the mother-loving spiders.

But there it was. A bark. Out of time, out of rhythm, the

wrong pitch. It shouldn't be there at all. It was not a bark but a barking. For how could only one bark be heard in that vast space and amidst that glorious music? No, it was more than one and it was there and there and there. And there. The dogs were silent, still obedient, obediently still. And silent. The barking was from the people. Gravel-and-grit voices of persons not used to speaking much, angry in tone, tremulous with the screwed-up temerity they had managed to induce in themselves and one another.

Here was the sound of one bark: "False gold!"

Here was another: "False transcendence!"

And another (and so strange a claim!): "False spiders!"

Emperor Scarble's upraised first set of arms (his original, from before the transformation), slowly came down to his sides. He no longer stood in Fingerling Salute to his children, his wayward and weird children. They had grumbled before, certainly. That was why he called them wayward. Imagine someone grumbling amidst such golden plenitude and perfection! Yet he had mother-patience with their perversity. But never in the assembly had any unplanned or unapproved noise been heard from them. Never on high holy carnival day. Not even in the earlier Ceremony of Stinkers where they all were allowed, for the grotesquery of it, to hold their noses as if they smelled something foul, had there been an undue noise heard. (The impossibility of a stink was what made that ceremony so funny, so carnival, so grotesque. Foul stenches had been extracted long ago at the coming of the Golden Transcendence. Everything came up smelling like a silk rose now.)

But this, this interruption of ritual with a very rough sort of— what was the word they used to use, a very ungolden, unsilken word—*creativity*, that was it (what need of sloppy Fingerling "creativity" when the mother-loving spiders had engineered all to completion?) and it was categorically *not* funny. This irruption of a very uncouth sort of "creative expression" in the already perfectly balanced ecology was unheard of. Well, it could be heard louder and louder now as the people's voices got a little less rusty and a little more in unison.

The New Spiders on the outer perimeter started to get report of this people-barking and their bolos and nunchaku and swords and switchblades and pistols started weaving and bobbing, shadow-slashing, ready to bite some real flesh-and-bone stuff, of the Fingerling variety. (The Aranean Spiders did not have the satisfying fleshiness and bloodiness of Fingerlings, should they ever—never!—have need to be cut down.)

The dogs themselves became uncertain, torn between loyalties. They broke silence here and there with whimpers.

The singing of the Aranean Spiders began to break as the weapon-wielding New Spiders shouldered past them to wade into the center of the gathering, where the soon-to-be-bleeding Fingerlings were standing with their food-dogs.

Emperor Scarble, now having ascertained the situation, acted decisively at once. He clapped his middle four sets of hands together, the New Growths of Transcendence. The sound was amplified just as his voice had been so that the clap was a thunderclap. This motion from him brought each of the fractally scattered eidolons together into the center of the gathering in an instant. When they were thus united, they formed a single eidolon of the Emperor that was now the size of the many put together, a figure so gargantuan its head seemed to touch the sky, a skyscraper Scarble towering over them. The sight defied ocular intake. But the barking people weren't really paying any attention to the sky anyhow. They appeared to be looking down now, slapping or brushing at something on their knees perhaps, some of them getting down to the ground and thumping it once or twice. And the barking had changed to some other even rustier sound that hadn't been heard once this past year (not in the open anyhow). It was not a golden or silken sound and had no place in a complete world.

The sky-high eidolon of Emperor Scarble itself bent down low over the Million, his gargantuan face coming down out of the sky and peering at the great crowd over which it hovered. On the imperial platform, Emperor Scarble himself was bent in a mirror of that motion. He too appeared to be peering at the ground, his lowest pair of arms bracing himself with hands on knees as he squatted.

But the two motions were unconnected. The people, the children, were doing one thing and the Emperor another. The similarity of their down-peering aspect was incidental. As the New Spiders began to descend upon the great gathering of children to put an end to this ungolden irregularity, they saw that the peering at their feet and the slapping at both knees and ground had no object. The people, the children, peered and slapped at nothing. (The Original Spiders, the arachnids, had scattered quickly out of harm's way at the very beginning of this display.) Indeed, many of the children's eyes were closed or unfocused. And many of their mouths were hanging open, while others were tightlipped but fit to burst, and some began slapping at each other, backs and shoulders clouted, and some hugged and stumbled upon each other. And what, what, what was that sound they were making, so long unheard? It was a kind of barking, but not like their first outburst of negations. These new barkings were more like affirmations. As the New Spiders made their first cutting and gunning blows, they suddenly recognised the sound. It was one they had made in their old life, before the Night of the Great Hatching. They hesitated at the submerged memory, having shed only a little of the children's blood.

On the imperial podium, Emperor Scarble was doing none of this, but was, rather, peering down at actual, visible objects, a growing swarm of them, in fact, a skittering stampede of Original Spiders pouring up the cliff and up onto the platform. The arachnids pooled and eddied about his feet and fanned out from him covering the entire imperial dais-podium. A line of them swarmed up his back inside his robes and onto his neck, deftly unfastening the robes, letting them fall to the ground.

"Yes, my subjects," he said, a little shakily, "perhaps I should be unencumbered in this unprecedented moment."

Then they tipped him. They piled right under his feet and tipped him over onto the waiting backs of their fellows, and they thus began to carry him away.

"Yes, my cousins, yes. Perhaps it is wise at this unaccountable juncture," Emperor Scarble said, still a little more shakily. "Take me to my chambers."

But they took him to no such place. Or rather, they took him to his new chambers, where he would reside for an eon, dodecapodic bones licked lovingly clean and made the home of various hydrophitic and crustaceous families for generations.

As the Original Spiders whisked the Emperor off the platform and across the terrain to the cliff's edge, his giant eidolon went sliding across the sky out from over the heads of the people, the children. Some noticed and maybe laughed a little harder.

Laughed?

That was it. That was that sound, it came to New Spiders now, and they knew it was wrong, very wrong in such a right world. But somehow it did not enrage them. It was hard to get mad at a million people having such a frank and cathartic laughing fit. The weapons drooped and nearly dropped from many of the New Spiders' many hands. And then something else was happening to their hands, the ones that dangled low down at their sides anyway. Wet, warm sandpaper was being applied in swift repeated strokes to their palms and fingertips and the backs of their hands. They very nearly smiled at the strange, long forgotten sensation.

The dogs, the children's food, were licking the New Spiders, the Other True Adults, the transformed humans, licking them in renewed love and loyalty. The dogs had not forgotten, not entirely. The dog's finally knew where their allegiances lay. They began to bark their own doggy laughter in contrapuntal chorus with their people, the children. The New Spiders half-heartedly killed a few of the dogs. But it didn't bring the usual bright screaming pleasure to their veins. As they had watched, a moment ago, their Emperor dragged on his back across the sky above their heads, they felt their direction and resolve slide away too.

And this is what had happened. One of the people, the children, had told a joke. It was not a good joke. In fact, it barely counted as one. It was as rusty and raspy as their voices, for it was a very out-of-practice practice. But it was enough to do the trick.

The joke was this: "What did the girl do when the spider proposed marriage to her?" The answer to this set-up is variously said to have been "She cut her eyes at Spider Face" or "She turned up her nose to Spider Face" or "She curled her toes to Spider Face". It was not good, it was reaching, it was barely groan-worthy. But it was based in a real event. It was in the direction of political satire. And it did the trick. It broke the golden web, it cut the silken cord. Things were no longer perfect. And without perfection, why, anything could happen.

And it did. The people laughed, the dogs barked out of turn, the New Spiders hesitated to kill, the Original Spiders revolted against their Proconsul, and the Proconsul, the Emperor, for his part, drowned.

But the Aranean Spiders reacted according to plan, always according to plan, to benign design, to the engineered pre-ordinance. Rebellion must be put down. The Level Perfection must be rebuilt at any cost. The Araneans resumed their singing, but now of a different song, to the tune of the Lulling Warfare, and they shot their silk as they sang in a flossy glossolalia, angelic overlords pouring out a cataract of mother-loving lyrics and melodies.

Millions of nearly invisible streamers coalesced into filmy visibility and caught at the people, the children, and their food, the dogs, and their adult masters, the New Spiders. The people's laughter ceased in some quarters, became muffled and sticky in others. The dogs' barking and licking much the same. But the New Spiders, the transformed humans, at last knew what to do. Their ten weapon-wielding limbs rejoiced again at the prospect of mutilation and maimery, but now directed toward a new object and objective. Bolo knives and switchblades and swords and machetes and pistols and glocks slashed and fired at the webworks falling from the sky. They hacked the silk to bits.

And now the people, the children, found yet another recension of laughter, even more rare and forgotten than the knee-slapping guffaws they had already rekindled. They recognised the New Spiders not as their mothers but as their brothers, their sisters and friends and comrades - and, indeed, their mothers, fathers, children, families of old - and the tears stung into their eyes at the same instant the laughter of recognition and joy leaped off their tongues. Tears of laughing joy.

So the Aranean Spiders had to get down into the fray. The overlords had to close ranks with all these wayward children and backward adults. They had to bite their mother-love into them anew. The people and the people, the children and the neo-spider adults, were ready, however, to bleed. Rivers and rivers of their very own costly blood would be preferable to the silk-fine and hollow Golden Transcendence they had been dozing in this long while. They were ready to wake up and bleed again. The happy ferocious dogs beside and inside the people leapt forth, from the people's sides and from their eyes and their battle-laughter. And the Original Spiders and the New Spiders joined in joyous purpose too. The wolf spiders and lynx spiders and hunters and jumpers and all the rest came leaping from the sky and ground and from out of the blazing eyes of the transformed humans.

-

"But..." said one of the people, the children, uncertainly.

"But," said another, taking it up, "the weapons of our warfare are not carnal!" This person mused a moment, then added: "Are they?"

Likeminded questioners began to find each other as the battle started to engage. Whatever their views on the necessities or evils of war, these small groups began to kneel to the ground here and there all across that mile of the Million and they performed the strangest ritual this day had yet seen, a ritual more forgotten and forbidden than laughter, though it had only been underground, not unpracticed. They supplicated, interceded, made request. (*To whom? To whom did they make request?* Ah, we'll not be so graceless or inelegant as to say it outright.) They prayed for deliverance from their oppressors and yet also for the forgiveness of those same oppressors. They prayed for reconciliation with Araneans and a just peace. They pleaded a Blood more ancient than these enmities.

-

And in such commingling of silk and blood, of Gold and Crimson, the Perfect World ended.

-

Did the children and the New Spiders prevail over their Aranean usurpers and overlords?

Be quiet. We watch.

Did the thing spread? Did the joke, the laughter, reach from the engineered Gold-and-Green Fingers out across the ocean to other continents? Was it met on the way by fingers of laughter reaching back toward it from the other side of the world?

Be quiet. We wait.

Was the face of the Earth renewed from its cobwebbed false-golden lethargy then? Did a new rump and face come ruddy and puling out of that broken, golden shell of a world? Did genuine transcendence finally appear and obtain, not the Levelled Plateau but the Rampant Dimensionality?

Be quiet. We hope.

*T*o you who are scattered and broken, gather again and mend. Rebuild always, and again I say rebuild. Renew the face of the Earth. It is a loved face, but now it is covered with the webs of tired spiders.

R. A. Lafferty, "And Walk Now Gently Through the Fire" (1972)

THE PRYBAR SPIEL
by Noah Wareness

I've always got the nicest people cornering me at parties,
listing off my literary influences. It always turns out I
haven't read any of my own literary influences, so I'm not
sure where I stand in relation to Saint Laff, the Only One
Who Doesn't Know Everything. I usually say Lafferty when
they press me. I say the thing about how he rolls the
different styles together as one, the Golden Age sf burlesque
and the indigenous-styled mythtelling and the tall tales.

I'm really not sure where I stand. One thing they never
mentioned in four years of creative writing class, you should
write about what you care about, so you stay interested.
Insofar as writing's a way to learn about something, it goes
off at a crazy angle to writing what you know. I spent the
last six years writing a fantasy novel about hardcore punks
— I went to a lot of punk shows when I was a weed-
smoking teenager, and nobody would talk to me. It's funny
because if the community had let me in back then, I would
have realized the kids in the mosh pit were just weed-
smoking teenagers with different shirts than mine, and there
wouldn't have ever been a book. Hardcore wouldn't have
ramified in my mind to eventually become its mythological
backbone.

"Mythological backbone" is a phrase the saint's ghost taught
me to use.

I might be the only person who got into punk rock by

writing a book about it. In the process I made friends with enough punks that I found myself inside a community. Bands play in my living room, I've fixed my jacket in forty places, we're getting half our food from the grocery store dumpster down the way, and now that the book's done I'm binding copies in my basement because dealing with a third-party publisher feels profoundly like a surrender. One of these days I'm going to meet the saint's ghost on my deathbed, and he'll tell me about that one time my living room became some kind of time-voyaging superposition of the Catholic Church for three whole hours, and I could have gone with them if I just yelled the right utterance.

Eric Walker said that, with Lafferty, "the story you are reading is never the story he is telling" — that the works are powered mainly by interactions between highly specific symbols drawn from the works of ancient historians and theologians. I'm attracted to this model because judging from Lafferty's incredible erudition and his frequent, sour attacks on run-of-the-mill humanity, it's probably pretty accurate. Also that it implies I don't understand a word of my own favorite author's work. I'm pretty excited by that second part — what was I saying about literary influences and the hardcore scene?

I will say that my friends are very, very smart, and they never give a shit when I'm trying to make a story mean something else. Also that the story ideas that stab our brains at night invariably seem to be surface-level ideas. (What kind of deep reading improves the nightmarishness of a nightmare?) But Gene Wolfe said this thing once that I never finished figuring out. He was talking about how we think we invent symbols, but really it's the other way around. How symbols shape and define us without our intervention or consent, and we don't need to know about them for it to happen. The saint said something even weirder on the topic of symbols, though. He said we're trapped inside them, screaming to get out.

I suppose that's my explanation for why a story's here with no specific relation to Lafferty's work except for the one desperate six-year-old allusion roped to its prow like a humongous paper-mache lobster. I'll never be able to honor him by meaning to, no more than anyone can live up to the voices inside their head. But this project exists in large part because Lafferty seems to be speaking from another dimension — clearer and even somehow closer than this one — which is our actual home.

Other writers are influences. Lafferty is a revelation. The ordinary world's not even paper and there's ghosts reaching in every second, but you try and tell that to a party. You turn from where you're scanning the bookcase and tell them about cracking open your own femur, looking for the red strand.

PS. The story here is a folk myth from what they call Lost Angeles, told by the last punks in the world.

- Noah Wareness

Back before all that shit went down and the punks had to take it to core, a crew we all know found a cheap house on the edge of the park, and they lived there for a couple of years. There's not any rules left, but we still go there whenever we diy. And it was the House of the Unfinished Basement, right, and the House of All Ways In. This is the joke of how it all began, and the house was called Anything Goes.

They stood sticks in the dirt til tomatoes grew. They pulled down a wall in the basement and did shows. Punker'd jump from the washer and dryer into the crowd. They had a dumpster copymachine they fixed with the guts from a lamp, and they'd truck it around in a sideless shopping cart, back when the roads were flat as your hand, so if your crew wanted to do zines they'd bring it out. They had to flush the parrot when it broke its skull fighting the window, and then they got fucked on sugar cider and packed eight kids into the shitter, stuffing the corpse down with a mophandle and watching the feathers float up. They put the sofa up on phonebooks, punks sleeping underneath, and in the bathtub they made chowder and smokebombs.

You weren't there.

When things broke down they'd get together at the kitchen table and spread out some library books, or trade favors with somebody who knew the trick. So the wind never got in under the windowframes, and the power never jumped off the wires and cooked anyone, and whenever somebody's elbow broke the plaster, they both got patched. Spaces kept going under, but they kept it together at the House of Anything Goes, and the shows got really hard. On Groundhog Labor Boxing Day somebody went assfirst through the only wall standing in the basement and left a hole shaped like a dirty punk.

Couple nights and they had a wall fixing party. Everybody was broke so they pried twobysixes off a halfbuilt pizzahut. They took bikes out to the desert and dug around for gyprock to mix a bucket of plaster. When the patch was up they stuck their fingers in the wet plaster and carved FEAR and GERMS CIRCLE ONE. They carved AGNOSTIC FRONT, MDC, BAD BRAINS. Then somebody took a hammer and beat a nother hole in the wall. Said this patch we made, it's the only diy part of this whole fucking wall. And somebody else grabbed the hammer. They were like, what's wrong with your hands?

So the wall fixing party crew shoved their hands up the house's asshole. They used their knees and headbutted and jumpkicked the framing apart and in their chaos laughter bit chunks off the drywall till nothing stood but one plaster patch like a gutter punk's gray soul flying backward. Then the ceiling caved in. They fucked off to the backyard and had a lot more shine, and everybody slept that night with their drunk jackets on.

Spaces kept going under. There's no good times for hardcore, and Angeles was an oldschool city, with laws instead of hands. They'd come by a hall and say this doorway's too narrow, we're shutting you down. Or they'd say, your backyard's got too many old mikeywaves and your shower water's piss. We're pushing it down with a backhoe. Don't ask us bout it. We're actors of the law.

But their hardcore stood all around them in the House of Anything Goes, under the couch cushion stains and under the sink and their nails, and as they lived there so would they diy. That morning they made coffee and tactics. They hauled out the busted part of the kitchen floor, skinned a silkscreening table with the lino and stacked the wood outside. They nailed up a plank ladder and it turned out decent actually, with smooth basement-to-kitchen access. So they ate pancakes, and their meeting bout fixing the floor pit, it went into a meeting of what pit to build next.

They had to diy every day, the hardcore of the house called it, plus everybody was still broke. But they started arguing over a prybar. It was brand new with the sticker on, it cost tires and tires worth of money at the shop where they stole it, and it could of really ripped into the upstairs hallway floor. But the morning was still pretty early, and some punks were saying things like what good's a prefab tool anyway? We can't mooch off stores forever. Let's use this one for wiping ass and diy a tool out of our hardcore that's ours.

At the dump they found a huge lump of concrete stuck through with cast iron pipes. That night they pushed it over an overpass to bust the concrete off, and ground an edge on the biggest pipe with a stick of rebar as a file. They were all set to yank floorboards, but it was pretty late by then. They might not of been thinking straight. We recovered this pipe, somebody said, but business had it first. This shitpipe from a yuppie prison. It's got too much baggage. If we're serious for getting ready, we can cast a prybar from scratch.

So they snapped the rest of the iron pipes against a road divider, so they could all fit in this old propane grill. They took snips and wrecked the venturi tubes to let more propane in, and grilled the iron at a million degrees in a big steel pan. They put some olive oil and lemon on the molten iron, with a lot of black pepper, and poured it into a mold diyed from a log.

They all sat drinking gatorades while it cooled. Getting up every couple minutes to squeeze out piss on the red iron. Then somebody said hold on. Sure this is hardcore, but big industry ripped this metal out of the ground and they left a poison crater. We can mine our own ore. Diy hardcore carbon steel.

That night they looked in the front of the phone book for hematite deposits, and called some friends with couches on the way. They scabbarded shovels on bike carts and put trailmix in jars. They hitched up to Redding, where the river's stained pink with tailings, even today. It was three days to hitch to Redding, back when the roads were as flat as your hand. They cut the fences round the bandoned mine and climbed scaffolding down to the pit, and filled two duffel bags with the reddest rocks they saw. Rolled them back onto the #5 in a wheelbarrow from an old equipment shed. Then an unemployed horse truck took them home.

They were priming the barbecue smelter when somebody else started talking. We think we're hardcore for this? Ripping off sloppy seconds from the shittiest iron mine in Kaliforonia, that's scavenging, that's not the way of diying.

Somebody said we cant diy this any further than ore. Some nother punk said steel's just iron and carbon molecules. Real diy's building your own steel out of molecules. Somebody else said no, fuck molecules. Fuck molecules. Atoms are the hardcore of hardcore. We gotta take it to the atom smasher at UCLA.

So everyone put on the patchiest shit they had, sept for one tricker in a lawyer suit with a badge from the sal-mart. They partied at the atom smasher door with plywood grievance signs, yelling science would blow up the world. Then the tricker held up his badge and threatened the crew with a table leg. He said you're detained. You're detained on my authority and I'm taking you to detention.

The laws at the door figured it must be official. Everybody got through after that. They punched noses all around to get blood going, so it looked like the anarchy was under control, and when guys with nicer suits came through they ducked behind some shelves. In the control room they punched up some carbon for starters, cause it came first in the periodic table poster. Sirens went off, and there were some explosions from atom smashing, but they couldn't find how to turn off the carbon. So they took a piece of diy carbon from a burning wall and hotfooted it through a fire exit.

After that, they were planning their iron run back at the house. You know it. Punker stood up. Either way, we'll be using lectrons and shit from the McReagan ministration, and probly they were part of nazis before that. If we just diy a nother universe straight outa sweet fuckall we won't have to piss around with the laws of physics. Fuck laws and fuck the laws of physics. With an anarchy of physics we can diy every time we pull air and always be new.

Some punk said what are we talking bout? We already got three prybars.

Now we do. You're fucking welcome.

Noah Wareness writes weird fiction and poetry and hates author bios. He lives in a big house of friends in Toronto. You can read his stuff at noahwareness.tumblr.com.

THE WOMAN WHO WONDERED WHAT ONIONS THINK

by J Simon

Andrew Sandtherm was a practical man. He liked mechanical devices, particularly those with shiny metal and flashing lights, machines which sparked and clanked and tended to go berserk at odd moments. His inventions were flawed but profitable, a proposition his new corporate partners had no difficulty embracing, and his machines promised to make life very much easier indeed. It was all faintly miraculous, given the lad's unorthodox upbringing.

* * *

There had been an unspoken understanding that Andrew Sandtherm was a peculiar child. He was clever enough, to be sure, if a bit addle-minded: Easily amused, easily distracted—and almost unconscionably good at making things. Such as the contraption he built when he was three, a bewildering cat's-cradle of string and pencils using rulers as levers and toy trucks as counterweights which attached to the front doorknob and chimed warning whenever the Child Services people came to visit. Not that he cared who visited him, but the adults seemed pretty keen on being forewarned so as to keep the facts of his case from prying eyes.

It wasn't that Sandtherm's parents didn't love him; but there was little place for diapers and sleepless nights in their otherwise free and satisfactory lives. And so they offered the child up, on loan, to their fellows in the greater arts community. Oddly enough, it worked. There were any number of retired set designers who couldn't resist a baby, and then (as he grew older) plentiful musicians who found a toddler compelling, and finally (as he grew older yet) numerous college students and actors who relished the opportunity to leave their mark on a young boy's impressionable mind—enough so that he never did go to school. Andrew Sandtherm was raised by some four to five dozen parents and came to be a bit addled as a result, though he never seemed to mind the negligence to which he was subjected. He was too busy building things.

"Papa, can I be a musician like you?"

"No, son. You haven't the talent. But you can be the next Stradivarius. His art, his soul, were in every violin he ever made: What can you build for me?"

Young Sandtherm, now eight, spent months taking violins apart, studying them, measuring them, quantifying every detail with millimetric precision. He had to learn mathematics and woodcraft, along with the physics of sound and just enough Italian to read the older journals of the Art, but soon enough he was able to fashion a peculiar hybrid waffle-iron sort of machine which stamped out mathematically perfect violins by the score. He imposed upon his then-father to play, and listened; and when it was over, he gathered all the instruments along with their machine and quietly placed them in the trash. The sound had been perfect, but without warmth, without feeling. Some crafts, the young boy decided, must remain uniquely human.

* * *

Sandtherm's college years had been years of frustration for his many corporate suitors. He remained a student, and studied, and occasionally created a device of astonishing usefulness for whose design a corporation or two would offer a few million dollars. He invariably declined.

"What, my geologic analyzer?" he asked with a self-deprecating smile. "A little primitive, perhaps, but I've no plans to go back to it. It works, for what that's worth: I'd have nothing to learn by building another. It didn't discover any major new cavern systems to explore—nothing but petroleum and mineral deposits I wasn't interested in at all." He nodded politely as they offered employment, power, wealth. "I'm afraid not," he said reasonably. "Taking a job would involve leaving here," he said, indicating his shabby university office. "Adult life in the corporate sector seems designed to hold people apart. Alone. Disconnected. I'd rather stay here and enjoy this last bastion of community, this curious little tide pool of personal interaction. But please do take a mint on your way out."

The corporate executives persisted, convinced these sorts of statements indicated an utter naivete that might somehow be exploited. They didn't know, of course, about his nineteenth mother.

* * *

When he was eleven, Sandtherm came to live with an older couple, the woman a theatre-director whose children had grown. Her plays were not musicals, nor light farce. Sandtherm had many questions, his philosophical education having been sadly neglected to this point:

"Maman, why do bad things happen to good characters? And why does the audience come and see such awful things?"

"Because we've tricked them," she replied. "It's a good play and a good story, so their attention is captured by the time we give them bad things to watch. Not all plays are for fun, Sandy; Some are for showing things about life. Maybe those who watch will learn something. Maybe they won't. But they won't complain, not if the play is good."

Intrigued, Sandtherm decided that this must be a variety of paradox—that good could be used to trick people into accepting bad, and bad used for its own devious purposes—but when he built a machine to explore the concept, it lied to him and stole his lunch money. He decided that any further experimentation should wait until he was older.

For the next five years, Sandtherm quite happily allowed himself to be passed from artist to artist, prima donna to prima donna. He learned history from the first-chair violist, science from the operatic soloist, and grammar (including a choice selection of four-letter diction) from the lighting technician. For five years, he honed his expertise at making things, things of beauty, craft, and care, though he never did quite settle on just what it was he wanted to make.

* * *

Some two decades later, having finally agreed to put his talents to the service of Holy Profit, it was an older and wiser Sandtherm who settled down to work. He started by replacing fast-food workers with his devices, to the general betterment of mankind. His machines were efficient, cost-effective, didn't mind the drudge-work, and poured the gelatinous goop known as "shakes" in a harmonious symphony of coagulated artery-desecration. Never again would a patron have to make awkward personal contact with an unaesthetic, unpredictable human being. Of course, there were protests—what to do with those displaced from gainful employ?—but the problem sorted itself out sooner rather than later. As part of the new order, Sandtherm had devised an aerial delivery system to free the public of their need to visit restaurants at all: Strictly speaking, the catapults weren't entirely necessary, but no one else could figure out how to change the programming.

"You have to take the good with the bad," Sandtherm said when interviewed, a half-smile playing at his lips. "Robots must go berserk. And shakes must sometimes hit the family dog at sixty miles per hour. It's in the equations."

And so, each time a Shake Incident occurred, several shiny and almost-not-quite-likely-to-go-berserk machines were immediately dispatched to present the victim with a cleverly worded note of apology. This did not go over well. Eventually, the corporations had to hire back all of those unaesthetic, unpredictable employees to go into each neighborhood and make apologies, to comfort little girls distraught over the unexpectedly sticky condition of their pets and to generally make friends in the community so that no one would sue. Many a former fry-vat operator had reason to curse Sandtherm's name during the long, underpaid dinners and parties and games that inevitably seemed to come up with their new client/neighbor/friends. Sandtherm, himself a veteran of the industry, had little sympathy for their plight.

* * *

After more than a decade's reliable service, Sandtherm's old cat's-cradle machine had finally broken down (a single string having worn away and snapped), and the young boy's deplorable life of horrific neglect was discovered. He went willingly when they came to take him away, for he had learned over the years that old friendships never died, and he was eager to bring his talent for creation to a grander stage. Fortunately, the state had a similar purpose of mind: For, while Sandtherm—at sixteen—was too old to be easily placed in a new home, he could at least recover his dignity and pride through honest work and earned wage. He soon found himself gainfully employed, part-time, at the local burger joint.

"Press the button until the light goes on," the assistant manager explained. "And when the light goes off, empty the fries into this bin."

Sandtherm nodded, genially befuddled. "My job seems to consist of only sixteen distinct instructions," he noted, "which combine into only five greater tasks. I deduce that this job has intentionally been kept simple as a way of granting us enough free time to pursue other arts of our own volition... such as taking buns and re-arranging their sesame seeds to form alliterative haiku on the nature of being," he said hopefully, "unless that's already been taken?" His smile faltered as he saw the assistant manager's uncomprehending expression.

Sandtherm's employment began on a Tuesday. He loved the paper hats and enjoyed distributing cheap plastic toys to children, but never understood why he should be chastised for bringing his own jigsaw and his own potatoes to work, thence to cut the spuds into puzzles of three-dimensional intricacy and distribute them to customers at a rate of two potatoes per hour. Nor did he understand why he mustn't carry on lengthy personal conversations with patrons who were desperately trying to get in their orders before their lunch hours expired. Despite lengthy explanations to the contrary, he refused to believe that any job could truly be what he called "purely mechanical"—that it could be utterly devoid of the human arts of entertainment, comradery, or craftsmanship. "Always smiling, whatever we feel," he said after

one particularly frustrating session, "always politely curt as if to
end the painful experience of human contact as quickly as possible.
No independence. No craft. No art. What is there about this job
that could not be better performed by a machine?"

The manager, inexplicably, was unsympathetic. Gradually, day
by day, they broke him of these habits, forced him to perform his
sixteen instructions and his five tasks. On occasion he still let his
mind drift, or walked stiffly about making little buzzing and
clanking noises, but no one seemed to notice.

* * *

Sandtherm's corporate backers, pleased by the success of his
food-service mechanization, strongly urged him to continue. And
so he did, replacing telemarketers with sales-devices which rapidly
malfunctioned and became so persistent, so persuasive, so utterly
and unconscionably cruel that no human could speak to them
without being reduced to tears. Sandtherm tried mightily to disarm
the machines (or so he claimed, though he seemed to choke
slightly as he did so), but they had somehow been granted the
ability to burrow deep under the earth and tap into the global
communications network from a distance, their brilliant evasive
tactics and seemingly limitless self-replication ability assuring
humanity a constant barrage of sales harassment until the end of
time.

"I don't know why I built them that way," Sandtherm told a
hastily convened congressional committee. "It seemed like a good
idea at the time. Sadly, there's nothing I can do to stop them."

And he said it with a straight face, too.

Eventually, the only thing that could be done was to take the displaced telemarketers and any portion of the population who could be spared—largely volunteers from among the unemployed elderly—and train them as therapists to visit and care for those who had suffered such attacks. Understandably, a burgeoning pro-Human movement also sprang forth in opposition to Sandtherm's improbable inventions, and to protest the mechanization of such uniquely human jobs as asking "do you want fries with that?" The former marketers found themselves bent to unnatural tasks of intimacy and care, things better suited to family and friends than to displaced salesfolk. Sandtherm, a veteran of their industry also, muttered a few sympathetic words but said little else.

* * *

When he was seventeen, Sandtherm found work taking orders for a mail-order catalogue. By this time, he had held—and lost—many jobs. He had learned. He had changed. Mostly, he knew that he might not have another chance if he wanted to make enough money to start college. He was determined to try his best to do what his employers wanted. To be what they wanted. His customers, he knew, found their lives quite trying enough without having to ask a complete stranger for their porcelain dwarves and edible underthings: Indeed, they would rather have spoken to a machine. His initial impulse—that, if he conversed with them long enough, he would no longer be a "complete stranger" and might help them choose the gnome most appropriate to their lifestyle—he suppressed. Instead, he devised the Algorithm.

Sandtherm's algorithm for dealing with customers was a beautifully scripted flow-chart, an exquisitely sculptured harmony of lines and squares, triangles and arrows detailing every conceivable customer query and every conceivable response thereof. Each morning he rose well before the sun so he could take the hours necessary to painstakingly inscribe his famed Algorithm on whatever was at hand—an eggshell, a pancake, a stray turtle rescued while trying to cross the road—and every day he followed the Algorithm's every line and dictate. His customers, he knew, would rather have spoken to a machine. Many who spoke to Sandtherm were convinced that this was in fact the case, and he did not disabuse them of that notion.

* * *

Despite the debacle of the marketing machines, Sandtherm was permitted to continue with his inventions. The corporations which were profiting from his devices seemed oddly willing to continue buying them, even pushing him toward the highly lucrative areas— the so-called "human jobs"—he had once been reluctant to tackle.

He responded with automated child care devices (which had quite inexplicably been endowed with wheels and immediately took to chasing after children in packs, taking them captive and teaching them terrible things), quarter-operated psychoanalysts (see following), electric priests (which rapidly abandoned their original programs to team with the psychoanalysts and lurk together in dark alleys, calling deeply disturbing philosophical ideas to passersby unprepared to cope with such sophisticated invective), mechanized rest homes (about which the less said the better), and robotic nurses (who could be found distributing pain pills on the logic that hospital revenue could be greatly enhanced by frequent repeat visits).

"There are a few natural errors," Sandtherm admitted when confronted by an angry mob. "But I think you'll come to appreciate the ability of very efficient and almost not inimical personal care devices to ease your lives. After all, you have no other choice: not unless you want to take the practice of human care back into your own hands. And we all know how inconvenient that would be, don't we?"

Despite his glib explanations, it became almost immediately apparent that Sandtherm's machines were an invidious menace to humanity itself. The public backlash was swift and terrible: Militias were formed, entire communities coming together to roam the streets in heavily armed machine-hunting packs (although their rampage hours were necessarily limited by the need to remain home caring for children, elderly, wounded, and each other).

Sandtherm's machines had never been built to resist such brutal tactics, but—due to their self-replication abilities—their removal was an ongoing task. Understandably, a large part of the insurgency focused on the very large reward that had been placed on Sandtherm's head. Of those who searched, few had known him. And only one could say she had known him well.

* * *

In the wake of his various part-time jobs, Sandtherm found college an infinitely friendlier place. He buried himself deep in the machine shop and stayed there as one year passed into another, the school's records computers having long since forgotten whether he were junior or senior, grad student or professor. Having rebuffed the corporate scavengers and kept his machines to himself, he settled in for what was beginning to shape up as a very long and very nondescript life. Right up until he fell in love.

He didn't know quite how it happened, but Sandtherm found himself taken with an enthusiastic young journalism student, a not-entirely-practical lady who spent a disproportionate amount of time practicing her interviewing skills on cats (whose answers, she claimed, were invariably 'feed me') and doggedly hunting down answers to the sorts of questions that individuals less determined than herself may have dismissed as "rhetorical." Although terribly certain that she could never be interested in one such as him,

Sandtherm nevertheless paid court, giving her elaborate mechanical dragonflies that flew all of their own and inscribing heartfelt musings upon individual hairs collected from animals of various species. The young lady, having always harbored a secret desire to investigate the feelings of onions, found Sandtherm a kindred soul and quickly disabused him of any notion of her non-accessibility. For a time, all seemed well. For a time, his devices were mostly of a type intended for two. But then, upon graduation and receipt of her degree (as well as a ceremonial replica inscribed upon the hair of a capybyra), Sandtherm's lady-love took a position as a local news-anchor repeating the news she was given to say at five and at six, a slightly different version at eight-thirty, and the altered version again at ten. And always smiling. Always in the best of moods. She no longer felt like talking when she came home, no longer had time for so many of the silly little distractions they used to enjoy. And when she got her big break and moved on to the big city, she did not ask Sandtherm to join her.

Six months passed. A certain corporate executive received a phone call; the voice on the other end somehow being calmer, more mature than the last time he had heard it.

"I'm ready to come work for you now," Sandtherm explained. "There's really not much keeping me here any longer."

The deal was struck, money and facilities supplied. Sandtherm could make most anything he liked, so long as it was profitable. The corporations finally had what they wanted. And received more than they ever could have anticipated.

* * *

And so it came to war and the entire earth shook, or would have had the warriors not wasted so much time and passion practicing their new careers at the now-ubiquitous anti-Sandtherm community centers. Sandtherm, acting in his own defense, struck back with a battery of devices intended to disrupt global communications, but—almost predictably—his machines failed to work as designed and ended up disrupting only entertainment programming, replacing it with the hilarious computer-generated antics of Rhombus and Sphere; which, although graced with very high ratings among the television-watching machine demographic (as well as strong returns from "Who Shot Dodecahedron?" T-shirt sales), resulted in the indescribable calumny of forcing the maligned, overworked populace to take upon themselves the creation and performance of the arts on a personal, community-by-community basis. Oddly enough, people seemed to enjoy this sort of thing, and began to feel less need to watch the colloid of mayhem, fluff and sensationalism commonly referred to as the Evening News: Thus, Sandtherm's former love lost her job in broadcasting, the only alternative employment available, oddly enough, being onion-trauma therapy.

As much as she enjoyed her new profession, she gradually began to worry, wondering whether her subjects were naturally occurring or whether they had been artificially traumatized for the express purpose of creating this job for her. It wasn't the type of thing to concern a professional journalist, the idea of onions having feelings being laughable on the face of it, but she had more time to think, now. She did worry, and she decided—finally—to do something about it.

On each of her birthdays for many years, she had received in the mail a small box created as an astonishingly intricate three-dimensional puzzle of interwoven cardboard, a puzzle which—if it were to be unwound to a correct solution—would have taken hours or even days to unravel. She hadn't the time. She generally used a scissors. And the box, within, was always empty.

This year, however, she took the time to solve the puzzle from beginning to end, and didn't even mind when it turned out to be empty; but the time she took brought to her attention a detail that had escaped her over all the previous years.

There was a return address.

It was a small but elite party that went to brace the machine-making devil, yet a party that was growing rapidly smaller. Not a minute passed without someone's civil-defense anti-Sandtherm community beeper sounding and calling them off on some urgent task—a child under the sniper's care having stubbed her toe, a friend of the explosives technician wishing to share a particularly special sunset, the negotiations expert's wife having purchased an intriguing unguent, and yet others being called away on tasks better suited to jester or priest, artist or lover. Until, finally, she was left to brace Sandtherm alone.

The first door, built in painstaking precision from interlocking gourds, she tore down.

The second door, built from individually woven muskrat-hairs (on which were inscribed dryly acerbic comments regarding the paucity (Sandtherm had always loved the word 'paucity' but never understood its proper use) of tearing down muskrat-hair doors), she tore down.

The third was a machine which helpfully tore itself down as she approached. But the fourth—ah, the fourth, a work of satin and silver and hummingbird feathers whose stained-glass windows were fashioned of colored crystal fine as dust and applied speck by speck in such profuse detail of glorious celebration that she never could have brought herself to destroy it, never in a thousand lives or a million days. Fortunately, it was open.

"I feel it only fair," Sandtherm said, "To warn you that I have a very tasty cake of unusual type cooling in the freezer." He paused, seeming to think over what he'd just said. "But aside from that," he amended, "I happen to be carrying in my pocket an ultimate weapon of a type intended to destroy human civilization upon the moment of a button's press."

"There's no need for that," she said. "Fix your machines; Make them work as they're supposed to."

"Is that all?" he asked ruefully.

"You could hurry," she said, checking her watch. "I'm supposed to be tutoring the girls again this afternoon, and I need to get to the theatre for set-up well before seven. Just fix your machines. Let everything go back to the way it was before. That's all I ask."

"Then I should warn you that I happen to be carrying in my pocket an ultimate solution of a type intended to cause all of my machines to repair themselves completely and totally upon the moment of a button's press. And the cake will grow cold if we allow it to sit too long."

Distracted and bemused, she found herself asking, "What kind of cake?"

"Onion and orange. I let your cats—whom I apologize for kidnapping—select the ingredients by means of batting them with their paws. I put it in the freezer because I couldn't think of anything better to do with something so wretched. So. Do you wish me to press the button?"

When she was finished laughing, the woman who had once

wondered what onions think looked at Sandtherm, and at the device he now held in his hand.

"That's a machine, right?" she asked. "And you built it, right?"

"Are you calling into question the reliability of my devices?" he asked suspiciously.

"Push the button," she laughed, taking him by the arm, "and let's go see what cake my cats have made."

∞

J Simon is an author and programmer based in Wisconsin. He has recently published his first trilogy of novels, An Idiot Rode to Majra, Songs of Sa'bahr, and The Great Celestial Machine of Saithan (available at majra.org - check 'em out). Some years ago, he read Lafferty's "Eurema's Dam" in the Silverberg edited anthology The Best of New Dimensions. This story was the result.

OF CRYSTALLINE LABYRINTHS AND THE NEW CREATION
by Michael Bishop

"Of Crystalline Labyrinths and the New Creation" owes everything but its original maundering length to that cunning fantasist and oversized leprechaun R. A. Lafferty. When Virginia Kidd, then my agent, sent it to Robert Silverberg, a Lafferty admirer and the editor of the top-flight hardcover anthology series *New Dimensions*, Silverberg winced and called it a 'stunt.' Roy Torgeson, a Lafferty admirer and the editor of the second-tier paperback anthology series *Chrysalis*, proved more receptive and more gullible. He bought the story at almost twice its new wordage, ran it in the final spot in *Chrysalis 7*, and declared me in his introduction the author of the "only genuine lafferty ever written by anyone other than 'The Man' himself' " and as "a genius of sorts." (Punch *of sorts*.) In 1979, out of respect for a writer now shamefully neglected, I had written my so-called lafferty in high spirits, but what it really needed was a ruthless blue-penciling. Twenty two years later [in 2002] I've given it one.

Not long after I wrote the foregoing paragraph, Ray Lafferty died — on Monday, March 18, 2002, in Broken Arrow, Oklahoma. Although he allegedly stopped writing twenty years ago, Lafferty left to posterity some of the funniest stories and most lyrical oddball novels in the history of our field. In his hilarious novella *Space Chantey* (1968), he created a classic science fictional pastiche of Homer's *Odyssey* long before the Coen brothers transposed that story to the Depression Era South, as they do in their hit film *O Brother, Where Art Thou?* First published as half of an Ace Double, *Space Chantey* is now sadly out of print and exasperatingly hard to find. My copy disappeared from my shelves years ago. His major collections — *Nine Hundred Grandmothers* (1970), *Strange Doings* (1972), *Does Anyone Else Have Anything Further to Add?* (1974),and *Lafferty in Orbit*(1991) — feature dozens of his most inventive and flamboyant tales, but try to find any of them nowadays without recourse to the Internet. (Thank God for Lafferty's fans, who have done yeoman work to keep his memory alive.)

I have Lafferty's signature in two or three of my copies of his work, but I recall meeting him only once, at a convention in either Memphis or New Orleans. He had fallen asleep on a sofa in the hotel lobby, and his head had slumped forward, pressing his chins into his chest. As Jeri and I walked through the lobby, I paused to look at him and resisted with all my will an incongruous impulse to kiss his naked pate. Today, I wonder why I simply didn't do it.

-     Michael Bishop, 2003

There are multitudinous emanations, and sight is but one of them which is given us here in the childhood of the soul.

—R.A. Lafferty

1

Ossie Safire, character
A digger diligent and lean,
Went out one day searching for
Just one thalassapithecine.

Boomer Flats Ballads

Walking beside an arroyo on a gin-clear Oklahoma day, Ossie Safire caught sight of something: a shimmer, a shifting, *something*. Forty feet ahead of him, a shuffle of air and wind had just *unsparkled* in the gulch's clayey walls. By rockhound intuition Ossie knew that if he didn't hop down into the arroyo, whatever it was that he hadn't quite seen would disappear.

So down he hopped and strode up the arroyo talking to himself: "I'm looking for Osage pottery shards, the paleoliths of the enigmatic pre-people People, or the flipper bones and femurs of archaeo-okie thalassapithecines." (These last were seagoing ape folk of an undated inland-sea era in whom nobody *but* Ossie Safire believed.) "I am *not* looking for unsparklings of ostentatious air."

Rowdy Al LeFever had invited Ossie out to his ranch to look around. Rowdy Al, who hailed from Boomer Flats, claimed that a first-rate discovery lay in wait on his place for a dedicated rockhound. Ossie had met him earlier that day on the porch of his yellow, many-gabled, charmingly lopsided house.

"An unusual house, sir," Ossie had said politely.

"A fella down the road once tried to build one just like it," Rowdy Al told Ossie. "He said to me, 'Mr. LeFever, there is nothing so original as a first-rate copy.' The house he built fell over nine or ten times before he got one version to stand up. 'Well, it ain't an *inimitable* house you've got here,' he said, 'but I could've never built one anything like it without seeing yours first.' Later he tore it down and built a house more like himself, but I didn't think too ill of him."

"I've come to look for rocks," Ossie had said, trying to get back on topic. "Or fossils."

"Well, nose around. Make you a find. I've heard of you, Ossie Safire, and I want you to be the first to run across this thing." Rowdy Al had retired into his yellow house, leaving Ossie to his own devices.

And so, wishing for the serendipitous, Ossie stalked the thing he hadn't quite seen and fumbled his handpick out of his rucksack. A stand of cottonwoods topped the ochre rise beyond the arroyo's far bank. Ossie was admiring their long trunks and liquid leaves as all unexpectedly it happened, *it* being a collision.

"Ow!" he said. For he had bumped into an anomaly that would soon grow even more anomalous, and had scraped his nose. He thought he saw a not-sparkle – yes, a *not-sparkle* – interpose itself between his eyes and the cottonwoods. He lifted his handpick and tapped it on the motionless wind in the gulch, upon the airy hardness that his nose had bumped. The air blocked his handpick blow and shivered Ossie Safire's wrist. This is dismaying, he thought, for if no digger at the Greater Tulsa Diggers' Consortium can credit thalassapithecines, how may I hope that any of that crew will believe I have found a pocket of solidified air?

But Ossie, whom dismay seldom deterred, again tapped his discovery with his handpick. He tapped up and down and laterally. He tested the dimensions of the entire anomaly, which hung from unknown heights into the arroyo like an utterly transparent stalactite. Stooping, Ossie walked under its rounded tip. It had a radius of four or five feet and kept not-sparkling and not-glinting, all of which negative coruscations he now ignored.

(What *were* these unsparklings and not-glints? Ossie regarded the gin-clear day as one protracted flashing of the Cosmic Orderer; he thought the negative coruscations from the unseen rock winks of ordinary daylight. If this explanation sounds complicated, think how hard it was for me to devise.)

Ossie rued that he could not measure the *height* of the invisible stalactite. He threw dust on it hoping that a coating of grime might enlighten him, but the dust would not stick. It flew away on the Oklahoma breeze.

After a while, Ossie sat down on the arroyo bank with a peanut-butter-and-jelly sandwich and a flask of mineral water. He stared up at his discovery. Was this what Rowdy Al had wanted him to find? Apparently. And so it hurt that the huge, hanging rock would not be tricked into visibility. The Greater Tulsa Diggers' Consortium would expel him as a crank and a mountebank.

Eighty or ninety feet overhead, a graceful hawk collided with something and tumbled beak over pin feathers toward the arroyo.

Ossie jumped to his feet, but the hawk caught itself up and, flapping with clumsy flaps, avoided a crash landing only a few feet from Ossie's picnic. Groggily, the bird flew away.

A moment later, the brightness above Ossie unsparkled. Even more unsettlingly, he felt the invisible crystal *think* something at him:

Almostal comptured of omniversilly mattessence om Aye, O resiever of m'eye enconquerumphing metamorphilology.

This isn't fair, Ossie thought. I was hunting thalassapithecines, and this annoying weirdness isn't fair – not at all, not at all.

2

An Indian, called Flashing Plains,
Found a diamond on the prairie:
Sammy, blessed with spunk and brains,
Became a lapidary.

Boomer Flats Ballads

A week later in downtown Tulsa, Ossie Safire sat with three of his pals in the Arrowhead Lounge of the Diggers' Consortium: Ignatius Clayborne, whom everybody called Clay to avoid getting knuckled; Opalith Magmani, a beautiful beast of a woman to whom Ossie had proposed four times; and the richest Indian interested in archeology whom Ossie had ever met, Sammy Flashing Plains. All three wondered why Ossie had herded them together into this cramped Naugahyde booth.

"Which idiocy must we deal with today?" asked Ignatius Clayborne. "The pre-people People or your butterflying baboons?"

"Thalassapithecines," Ossie corrected his friend, humbly.

When Sharla, the barmaid, came to their booth to take their drink orders, Sammy Flashing Plains said, "No wisecracks about firewater, you guys."

Ossie ogled Opalith and said, "I'd like a dry Magmani." He quickly emended this to "A dry martini," his mouth chock full of the dust of chagrin.

They *all* ordered martinis. "Banish the vermouth," Sammy Flashing Plains said. "There's enough wormwood in the paneling."

"Well," said Ignatius Clayborne when Sharla left to fetch their drinks.

The frog in Ossie's throat croaked. "I've hesitated to talk to you all," he began, coughing a bit, "because of the esteem in which I hold all three of you: Clay, a geologist; Opalith, a stratigrapher, dendrochronologist, and reader of varved clays, not to mention the greatest beauty to come out of Tishomingo, Oklahoma; and Sammy, a—"

"Preservationist," Sammy Flashing Plains said. "I lead palefaces like you away from our holy places to do your digging, and I thank the Great Spirit that none of you is a social anthropologist." He sported a double-breasted blue suit and a headband of Osage design. Everyone else slouched there in work clothes.

"Okay," Ossie said. "Anyhow, out of esteem, I have hesitated to mention my most recent discovery. Now, though, several well-documented recent events have made it possible to broach the subject."

Their martinis arrived.

"What thubject?" Leaning forward in unstarched khakis, Opalith was a starching creature, alert and lissome.

Ossie turned his gaze upon his crystalline gin and recalled the matter at hand. "Have any of you all been reading the *World* or the *Tribune*, or watching the television newscasts?"

Except for Sammy Flashing Plains, who eschewed the media of the technocracy, they had indeed.

"Then," Ossie continued, "you have no doubt heard of the appearance, in diverse parts of the world, of sudden geological outcroppings."

"The invisible ones?" Opalith fingered her alluring tresses.

Ossie Safire nodded.

"It's a hoax," Ignatius said. "A convocation of world political leaders hope to take the public's mind off their manifold bumblings. Invisible outcroppings, indeed!"

"It isn't a hoax," Ossie said. "I've found one myself, one hundred and thirteen miles from here." He told his skeptical pals of the unsparkling on Rowdy Al LeFever's ranch and of how he had bumped his nose. Not one whit did he embellish, but he did refrain from mentioning that the invisible rock had communicated telepathically with him. (Well, *almost* communicated.) By way of epilogue he said, "Now there've been reports of similar anomalies as far away as Jerez, Spain, and as close as Dubuque, Iowa. I thought that maybe you wouldn't laugh me to scorn if I mentioned my own discovery in this context. Nine in all, there've been."

"I can add a tenth," said Sammy Flashing Plains, "but the report will be the most recent and the sighting the most ancient."

"Explain yourself, you indigent aborigine," said Ignatius Clayborne.

"That's *indigenous*," Sammy Flashing Plains said. "Which, in conjunction with *aborigine*, is redundant." He made his martini disappear. "Many years ago, when I was little more than what Clay would call a papoose, I saw just such an unsparkling as Ossie has described – a flicker on the sage-grown prairie. Little rib-ringed coyote that I was, I ran home shouting, *'The plains are flashing, O my mother! The plains are flashing, O my father!'* "

"Is this a retelling of the Chicken Little story?" Ignatius asked.

"No," Sammy said. "Incidentally, the proper name of that story isn't 'Chicken Little,' but 'Chicken Licken,' a fact having importance because of the incantatory nature of the poem's rhymes. These reports of invisible outcroppings may spell for us the same sort of disaster that overtook the protagonist of the nursery fable."

"We'll all by eaten by a fox?" Opalith Magmani said.

"Of course not," said Sammy, "but it's astute of you to recall the ending. What I suggest is that the incantatory nature of these reports may dull us to another possibility. Expecting a political catastrophe, we may fall prey to a totally different disaster – just as Chicken Licken, fearing skyfall, winds up as a fox's dinner. An important contrast does exist, however."

"Do tell," said Ignatius.

"Chicken Licken's error lay in supposing a universal catastrophe when she and her friends succumbed to a personal one. Our error may lie in assuming the collapse of a few local governments when the impending disaster will destroy *everything*."

"How fashionably gloomy," said Opalith.

Ossie Safire said, "What about your finding as a child, Sammy?"

"My father tried to dose me with castor oil, but my mother stopped him. She said that I'd seen only a bit of mica or tin can. I explained that I'd seen the unsparkling *above* the ground instead of *on* it, but they wouldn't listen. I went back to the prairie and found a jutting point of solidified air at waist height. I cupped my hands around it, but couldn't budge it. Finally, I draped my blood-red head cloth over it as a marker.

"When I returned the next day, my head cloth had blown into the sagebrush. I picked it out and, this time, *tied* it around the flashing crystal outcropping. But the cloth split and fell away again, for the rock inside my tiny bundle had . . . grown. I kept trying to capture it with cloth, but at last the rock point cut through the *blanket* that I had taken from my parents' bed. Then, friends, it spoke with an inside-out tongue of fire in my brain, saying *Tittle Smindian, you mayan't never trapture a manipphany of the Nu Cree Nayschun.*"

"Come again," said Opalith Magmani.

"That's what it said, inside me. I remember because *I* never thought like that, and still don't. My father spanked me for spoiling the blanket. The next day the outcropping vanished. Today I am a lapidary, a gemstone dealer, and an Indian even yet."

"An interesting story," said Ignatius. "Do you contend it has some bearing on what Ossie has told us about his own find?"

"Two plus two," said Sammy Flashing Plains.

Ossie Safire, grateful that Sammy had corroborated his account, downed his drink. He was also grateful that Sammy had recited the unseen outcropping's telepathic nonsense, for the recitation made him feel less crazy.

At least until Sammy said, "Twenty years ago, it wasn't time for what is going to happen to happen. Now, my friends, it is."

3

A bold quartet, they sallied out
Like buccaneers or reivers
To ask whose exegesis was most stout:
Why, Rowdy Al LeFever's!

Boomer Flats Ballads

Back out to the Oklahoma prairie they went, to the arroyo where Ossie had made his find – Ossie, Ignatius, Opalith, and Sammy Flashing Plains. Into the early-morning, blast-furnace swelter, one week later, they boomed along in Miss Magmani's jeepster. (Don't blame me if you prefer *Ms.* for the ladies. The *Miss* was Opalith's own idea, and she insisted upon it.) How that woman could wheel a vehicle. Her driving made poor Ossie wish for a headache powder or a fortifying tot of vodka.

If he hadn't known before, Rowdy Al now knew of his ownership of an invisible anomaly. He had invited four members of the Greater Tulsa Diggers' Consortium to visit his place to examine it. He would be waiting for them. And he was.

"Howdy!" Opalith hailed him, jouncing her friends up the drive to Rowdy Al's lopsided yellow house.

Out to the arroyo the rancher led them on foot. "Still here," he said as the five of them stared up at the big unflashing rock. He took off his Stetson, mopped his brow, and beheld the gin-clear Oklahoma sky. "A very quite anomaly," he said.

"They're all over now," Sammy Flashing Plains said. "From the Kirghis Steppe to the African Sahel to Ty Ty, Georgia, U.S.A."

"Twelve sightings in all," Ossie said. "Thanks for not publicizing this one."

"Well," said Rowdy Al, "it's been behaving itself."

"Any new developments," asked Ignatius Clayborne.

Rowdy Al pointed. "I think there's another one out in the middle of the pasture beyond those cottonwoods."

"Why do you think that?" said Opalith.

"The cattle have been crawling on their knee joints to lick the salt licks out there, and they don't usually do that. Also, it sort of winks."

"Have two outcroppings been 'seen' this close together before?" asked Ignatius.

"I don't think so," said Sammy Flashing Plains. "To avert catastrophe, we must determine the composition of these invisible rocks."

"Set up camp out here," Rowdy Al said. "Stay as long as you like." He pivoted on the arroyo bank and walked off toward his bric-a-brac-infested house. The whiteness of the day cloaked his dwindling bulk with a hieratic haze. O, did that man glow!

The others set up camp halfway between the hardness that Ossie had discovered and the one that Rowdy Al had hinted at. They soon verified that the second outcropping did indeed exist, a veritable floating mountain of invisibility, which they christened The-Anomaly-As-Big-As-The-Ritz. (Ossie's discovery, by the way, they called the Hope-It's-A-Diamond outcropping.) Its bottom hovered four feet from the ground, and it had the circumference of an oil-storage tank. Its height, no hawks having flown by, they could not even guess at.

Ignatius Clayborne set out stakes beneath the perimeter of The-Anomaly-As-Big-As-the-Ritz, strung the stakes together, and knotted orange rags to the string. He moved the offending salt blocks so that LeFever's cattle would not crawl over his pickets to get their licks in. Meanwhile, Opalith took soil samples from the area inside the flags, and Sammy circled the unseen rock trying to chip a specimen or two from its sides. Shivered wrists were all he got for his pains.

Ossie Safire hopped down into the arroyo and discovered that the Hope-It's-A-Diamond outcropping had grown. It had lengthened in parallel with the gully beneath it. If it kept growing, one day it would abut on the one where his friends labored. (The arroyo wound that way, you see.) Mazy walls of glass would divide the ranch as surely as barbed wire already did.

The moon jumped up, and they all retired to their stuffy tent. "Not a good start," Ignatius said. "What do you think The Ritz and the Hope-It's-A-Diamond are – invisible rocks, solidified air, or a flash-frozen liquid?"

"In this setting," Opalith said, "I would call those equally accurate, or inaccurate, ways of saying the same thing. The anomalies – which we cannot see, hear, or taste – occupy space, they encroach, and they grow. What does it matter if we call them rocks, air, or water?"

"Well, I'm a geologist," Ignatius said huffily.

"We can *hear* the anomalies," Ossie put in. "They ping when you tap them." He neglected to add that sometimes the rocks *thought* things at you.

"Still," said Opalith, "it's their space-occupying that frightens us. That, and their sudden popping into being, and their ability to grow."

That night, Sammy Flashing Plains rocked over his knees like a trance-taken medicine man. When Opalith dialed down the gas lanterns, the glowing gargoyles on the green tent walls faded from view. Talk mumbled off into sleep, and the night flowed down like embalming lava.

#

The next day, the four diggers resolved to delimit the transparent stones in space. The rag-hung cordons beneath The-Anomaly-As-Big-As-The-Ritz did this job inexactly. The flags kept them from banging into it, and the cows from crawling, but did not go far toward clarifying dimensions. Because the eroded gulch under the Hope-It's-A-Diamond made it hard to work there, the friends concentrated on The Ritz and discussed means and methods of plumbing its mysteries.

Ignatius said pontifically, "We must make this prairie-pent Gibraltar visible," and sent Opalith – who would allow no one else to drive her jeepster – to the hardware store in Boomer Flats to buy 1) an extension ladder, 2) a gallon of paint, and 3) a plastic bottle with a spray attachment.

"I got green," Opalith told Ignatius upon her return. "Your favorite."

Fortunately, he had asked for only one gallon because, once Ignatius had climbed the ladder and begun to spray, the paint – like the dust that Ossie had hurled on his first morning in the arroyo – would not adhere. Emerald droplets struck The Ritz's invisible surface and immediately slid or blew away. Ignatius, a many-freckled man, came down the ladder with a profane lack of grace.

"O Froggy," Opalith greeted him. "It looked so eerie to see you up on that ladder, balanced on nothing." And it absolutely had.

"We need a piece of canvas," Ignatius cried. "We'll wrap it, that unshpritzable Ritz. Wrapping large buildings was once a popular art form, and we can do it here, my band of brave upholsterers."

"It won't work," said Sammy Flashing Plains. "Don't you remember the story of my head cloth and the invisible rock point?" He said they should build a housing around the outcropping: a derrick-like structure or a series of scaffoldings.

Ossie noted that this strategy might prove dangerous, especially if the rock began to grow as they built.

"Then I'm going to ask Rowdy Al for some dynamite." Ignatius wrote a note to the rancher and carried it down the pasture to his big zinc mailbox.

That evening, in the gargoyle-haunted tent, Ossie's radio announced that new anomalies had made their presence known in Illinois, Texas, Nebraska, and Utah. Other parts of the world also reported more outcroppings. The four pals looked around at one another out of ash-colored faces.

Before going to bed, Ossie Safire walked outside and stood amid the cottonwoods looking toward Rowdy Al's house of many gables. All its lights were on, and jig music jogged up the rise to Ossie. Further, the silhouette of the heavyset rancher went dancing from one blazing window to another. Rowdy Al, it seemed, was rowdy in private, but you could participate at a distance in his genial rowdiness and commence to glow almost as bright as he.

Ossie crept back into his sleeping bag. To his disappointment, Opalith had again opted to sleep in work clothes.

#

On the third day they tried dynamite – a crate full of dynamite. On the top of the crate fluttered a tiny card whose handwritten message declared, *This is a good idea, but it won't work. R.A.L.*

It didn't work. Nor had the friends expected it to. (Still, you would have enjoyed watching Opalith and Ossie run off the cows.) However, the experiment blew up in their faces in a different way from what they had expected.

Beneath The-Anomaly-As-Big-As-The-Ritz, Ossie and Ignatius planted four separate charges. Then, after taking down their tent, they retreated to the arroyo, where everyone took cover under Hope-It's-A-Diamond. From the dusty gulch, they detonated their charges.

Whumpf. Whuumpf. Whuuumpf. And *whuuuumpf.* O, it was like a tubercular cow wheezing out the letters of a bovine Tetragrammaton. Afterward, the four diggers scrambled like lizards from beneath their rock to behold what they could behold and saw . . . well, nothing.

Or no more than several distended balloons of dust drifting hazily through the cottonwoods; those, and the orange rags that lay all over the land. As they came through the cottonwoods on their approach to The Ritz, they did see the outsized pothole beneath the invisible rock: a shallow crater, with lumps of dirt still lumpily in it, clods of clay that the wind had not dispersed.

Said Ignatius Clayborne, "Let's search for fragments."

Down on all fours went all four of them, with a few returning, cud-chewing cows looking on imperturbably. Ossie found blades of buffalo grass, sidewinder spoors, heat-steamed cow chips, and one crazily careening dung beetle. But he found no fragments of The Ritz, nor did anybody else.

"Such a shame," said Opalith Magmani, "such a shame."

They discovered, however, that they had altered the dimensions of The-Anomaly-As-Big-As-The-Ritz. Whole chunks around its base had disappeared, like bites out of an invisible mushroom.

"Those missing chunks," said Sammy, "have to be somewhere."

"Maybe they went back to wherever they came from," volunteered Ossie Safire. "Just like that rock point of your papoosehood."

"Uh-uh," grunted Sammy discouragingly.

"Explain yourself," said Ignatius Clayborne.

"Far from ridding ourselves of these invisible crystalline structures, if that's what they are, we may have facilitated their proliferation, growth, and ultimate imprisoning of the damnable human race."

"Boy," said Opalith, "you are one gloomy Indian."

Back in the vicinity of their dismantled tent, they listened to a National Public Radio announcer report new outcroppings in every state of the union, as well as in every country represented in the United Nations. Two streets in downtown Tulsa had filled with huge, invisible hardnesses, making them impassable; meanwhile, other cities had suffered similar inexplicable clog-ups. "We would say more," the announcer intoned, "but high-ranking government officials have asked us not to. Anyhow, it looks as if the *Rocks . . . Are . . . On . . . The . . . March."*

Ossie Safire wandered into the cottonwoods and stood looking for a long time at Rowdy Al LeFever's house. Tonight no lights blazed in the windows, no merry figure hippity-jigged among the rooms, and the house's yellow paint looked muted and muddy. Even so, the shingles on the roof had a phosphorescent sheen, and the spirit of Rowdy Al hovered spectrally over the landscape, more in control of things than he, Ossie Safire, would ever be. Things were falling apart; no, they were growing together, and something was not quite copacetic with the world.

The-Anomaly-As-Big-As-The-Ritz unsparkled under the moon like a demonic Ferris wheel. But it did not wink at him telepathically, and Ossie emphatically wished that it would. Comfort glinted in those ominous, rocky thoughts.

4

Strew flowers all about,
Heliotropes and hyacinths.
And let that yellow house draw out
Hosannas from the labyrinths!
Boomer Flats Ballads

They awoke the next morning to find that a wall of invisible glass had grown through the cottonwood copse. They walked out of their tent and went *bang* against it. Ignatius Clayborne collided first and then Ossie. Opalith and Sammy Flashing Plains escaped this indignity. None of them, however, could escape the implications of this new intrusion. Blasted fragments of The Ritz had taken root and bloomed into bulwarks, all viewless and vitreous where they didn't belong.

"Are we trapped?" asked Ignatius.

"No," said Sammy, "but plainly it has become dangerous to remain here. Look." Today, the wind blew hard, but the leaves and limbs of only half the trees around them jiggled. The others stood as if encased in Lucite molds – which, in a way, they were, for that clear rock stuff had flowed right around the old cottonwoods, fixing them fast. "This could have happened to us," Sammy went on, "and now we'd be nothing but four human aphids in amber."

"You're one eloquent Indian," Opalith said. "Shall we pack up and go?"

"A powwow," Sammy said. "Everybody sit."

In the stand of cottonwoods, an invisible wall on one side, they sat in a ring like pipe-smoking shamans. Ossie mused that he and his pals looked like picnickers at a feast of potential panic. How did it feel to have stone lap about you like gin and congeal, with nary an olive for comfort?

"I had a dream last night," began Sammy Flashing Plains. "In it, Rowdy Al LeFever told me that our anomalies are extrusions of a catty-corner crystalline vulcanism taking place in the continuum next door. A world over there is heaving and groaning and creating so abundantly that it's splitting its own seams. These extrusions, Rowdy Al said, are extropic in nature and may not soon cease."

"What's this 'extropic' business?" asked Ossie.

"Our system is an entropic one," said Sammy. "This other continuum runs on the opposite principle, one of endless creation rather than of unrelenting dysfunction and decay. Its system makes matter out of the great spinning Nothing, whereas ours can only . . . not destroy matter, but leach away at the old creation until it collapses.

"All this, and even more fabulous stuff, Rowdy Al told me as I dreamt. And as I slept, the crystalline lava of the New Creation flowed into our camp, lapped the trees, and lovingly hardened. It flowed through the seams that we had loosened with our dynamite, through the pressure points opened by the blasts that scattered abroad the shrapnel shards of The Ritz."

"So we've abetted our own downfall," said Ignatius Clayborne.

Sammy Flashing Plains ignored him. "The most fabulous thing that Rowdy Al told me was this: 'In the New Creation, Sammy, intelligence and nature have melded into an indivisible whole. The flowing lava and the seam-bursting crystal are blessed with sentience; they possess not only the ratiocinative ability but also imagination! They can recombine human language into more compact and meaningful units of ideation – *if only we could understand those units.* Rocks won't replace humans over here, but, instead, creative mineral *intelligences.* In such a domain, Sammy, death itself dies, for death can never conquer that which lacks frail flesh and frangible bone.' And Rowdy Al urged me to rejoice."

"In other words," said Ignatius, "using dynamite was a good idea except for the fact that it didn't work."

"It didn't work as we *expected*," said Sammy. "The downfall that Ignatius dreads holds embryonic life, and it would have occurred no matter what we did. Rowdy Al said, 'Sammy, as an Indian you see yourself as a constituent element of the world's adornment, not as a meddlesome observer with a trowel to poke at this and that. And that's good, for you're a part of the New Creation, too. You should daub on the peace paint and whoop the joy whoops, in awe and celebration."

"Rowdy Al's not your ordinary rancher," said Ossie Safire. "But how did he come to know so much about these invisible extrusions – when the world at large is so vastly stumped?"

"Rowdy Al," said Sammy, "has lived his whole life on the edge of an extrusion seam. When that seam, one of millions, finally flooded the earth with its faceted magma, Rowdy Al burst with power, too."

A quietness of great pregnancy sluiced around the four powwowing diggers, which Ignatius at length delivered of a confession: "I don't understand. And if that's true, what must we do today?"

"Walk among the walls and marvel," said Sammy. "This is the Last Day of the Old Procession."

And so the four friends walked out of the cottonwood copse, half of which stood imprisoned in otherworldly glass, and onto the undulant prairie. Unsparklings abounded in the gin-clear, blue day. The friends walked with their hands out, to feel where the Old World left off and the crystalline walls began. They walked down invisible corridors into unseen cul-de-sacs, marveling that The-Anomaly-As-Big-As-The-Ritz had mounted the sky, capturing midges, eagles, and clouds. Now it towered over woolly Oklahoma like a make-believe Matterhorn. Also, the Hope-It's-A-Diamond anomaly grew, shoving earth back from the arroyo bank as it snaked glassily along.

Aye anno feyk-meleaved usader intrurping mannakiddies' Dominuum, but the brightful peniheritariy of the Noocleation, tinkled the Hope-It's-A-Diamond outcropping as it expanded.

Meanwhile, The Ritz telegraphed this message into their heads: *Conseal Ur-shelves in the krowslege that ayn butte-iffal et plat-O-teaudinoose whey of execristence has come to Glas.*

And as the four explored the mazes around them, similar allusive thoughts poured like funny water from the rocks.

All the world over, Ossie told himself, this was happening. All the world over, the labyrinths grew. Meanwhile, he and his companions had become separated in their wanderings.

"You should know this about the extrusions, too," yelled Sammy Flashing Plains from a different maze pocket. "Their facets, no matter the angle of the matrix containing them, lie flush with every dimension of our continuum; thus, their invisibility." Sammy's voice sounded diluted and wan.

Ossie Safire, hearing this murky thinness, realized that he and his chums would never come back together – never in this life. Sammy Flashing Plains stood over *there*, in the middle of the plain, while Ignatius Clayborne knelt over *there*, down by the arroyo bank, while Opalith Magmani – that beautiful beast of a woman – waved to them all from the cottonwood copse. What a stately woman, favored of forehead, handsome of aspect, her hand raised in a gesture of triumphant valediction, for a fresh extrusion had recently captured her. Lost, but lost to him painlessly, for on the Last Day of the Old Procession they were joined in a marriage encompassing every living creature. He didn't even need to essay a fifth proposal.

Turning, Ossie noted that the Hope-It's-A-Diamond outflow
had engulfed and lifted up Ignatius Clayborne, who appeared to
float in midair, a man holding himself aloft by will alone, an angel
of latter-day geology.

Turning again, Ossie saw that Sammy Flashing Plains remained
animate and active, although he had shed his work shirt, baring his
breastplates to the sun. Now he stared into the white sky with
outspread arms and took small sacramental steps that led him
around in a slow, wheeling dance. He was one intent Indian, one
reverent creature among many of the Old Procession.

"Farewell, Sammy Flashing Plains," cried Ossie Safire.

He struck out through the unhardened plots remaining before
him, going where he had to go. Frozen cattle, suspended mesquite
pods, a jackrabbit caught in mid leap, and other monsters of eerie
delight broke upon his vision. Invisible walls funneled him this
way and that. He trod back down the ranch's whilom grazing area
and found himself in front of Rowdy Al LeFever's house. His
head ached with the manifold and mind-rocking thoughts with
which the labyrinth had just harangued him.

The lopsided house leaned. Its foundations no longer touched
the earth. White daylight congealed between the house and the
ground. Slowly, the house rose, as if on a column of translucent
fire. Ossie knew the column for an extrusion whose crystalline
body had sufficient power to obliterate gravity.

"Ossie!" a voice shouted. "Ossie, my lad!"

Rowdy Al LeFever clasped his legs about a lopsided gable of

the climbing house. He waved, and as Ossie Safire looked up, the rancher called down through the solidifying chasms. His burnished boots shot out stars of light. His face was refulgent.

"This is the New Creation, Ossie! And what you're seeing is only its magnificent leftovers, the excess and overflow of an eviternal birthing beyond our imagining!"

"But it's only rocks, Rowdy Al!"

"These rocks have life, Ossie. They're physical manifestations of the time-beyond-time in which that other creation is taking place. Look under my house, Ossie! You and Sammy heard them thinking, didn't you? In beginning of this world, as the Book says, was the Word, and likewise at the beginning of the New Creation. The Word is what fends off death, the Word is what creates, and right here on my ranch you can see the Word at work."

The house kept climbing, alarmingly a-tilt. It appeared to pull out of the very bowels of the earth an assemblage of unlikely, frozen-in-place creatures, which rose into the sky in ranks beneath the gaudy yellow house. Trapped in crystal, these creatures had come through the distended seam between continuums *from the other side*! A sea beast, a one-horned camel, a butterfly with three vulturine heads, a furry pterodactyl, all perfect and beautiful, rose in the ascending column.

"On the other side," Rowdy Al cried, "creation does not evolve. It self-evinces spontaneously, simultaneously, and everywhere. Whatever the mind may imagine, that you find there. Look again, Ossie. The sooner you do the better Sooner you!"

The house continued to ascend on its widening column, which displayed in an up-rush of solidified time-beyond-time its hard-to-imagine wonders – not fossils merely, but the things themselves. A family of the pre-people People, a school of thalassapithecines (hairy critters with prehensile fins and eyes like tarsiers), and fish with wheels. Whatever else Ossie saw, he forgot – except for Rowdy Al LeFever waving his Stetson in farewell and singing at the top of his inexhaustible lungs a cowboy paean in praise of the universe and its glorious abundance. And then the singing modulated into the telepathic babbling of the crystals as Ossie was engulfed and fixed for all time.

For here on the edge of the Order of Unbalanced Abundance, it was the First Day of the New Creation.

"Of Crystalline Labyrinths and the New Creation" from *Brighten to Incandescence* (Urbana, IL: Golden Gryphon Press, 2003), 201-215:

"Of Crystalline Labyrinths and the New Creation," copyright © 2002 by Michael Bishop. Significantly revised from its original publication in *Chrysalis 7*, edited by Roy Torgeson, Zebra, 1980. Reprinted by gracious permission of the author.

Story note on the piece by Michael Bishop as published in *Brighten to Incandescence* (see above for bibliographic info), 286-287:

Our eternal thanks to Michael Bishop for granting us permission to reprint this story!

THE SIX FINGERS OF TIME
- an essay by Andrew Ferguson

It's well known that sorting out R.A. Lafferty's estate has been, in legal terms, a mess. What's less well known is how "Six Fingers of Time" contributed to that mess.

For almost a decade, the Lafferty estate was a byword for snarled probate cases. Though he had a valid will leaving everything to his last surviving sibling, Anna, she died while he was in a nursing home. The several strokes he had suffered as well as his gradual deterioration into dementia meant he was not of sound mind to update the will; as neither Anna nor any other of Lafferty's siblings had children, this meant that his estate and literary rights passed to all his surviving relatives—and though Ray and his brothers and sister may have been unusual in their lack of issue, the rest of the family more than made up for this oversight.

The foremost task of Lafferty's executor was moving on the literary rights to a group better equipped to represent and propagate Lafferty's work. But thanks to the probate situation, every single heir (of majority age) would have to approve such an agreement: through extraordinary effort, they were just on the verge of one when something happened that spooked some of the heirs—or rather, got them thinking that they had hold of something much more valuable than was probably the case.

See, in 1994, Nicholson Baker wrote a novel called *The Fermata*. A film company bought the option, and hired Robert Zemeckis and Neil Gaiman to produce a screenplay. As is often the case, the studio also took out options on any intellectual property whose central conceit was near that of Baker's book—which was a protagonist with the ability to stop time and manipulate the people around him as he wished. Whether it was Gaiman, who certainly would've recognized the surface similarities to "Six Fingers of Time," or someone else who advised taking out the option, the result was a large amount of money being paid to the Lafferty estate to ensure that a movie would *not* made of that story, lest it encroach on *The Fermata*. Some of the heirs—a few of whom had heard of Philip K. Dick, or noticed that sci-fi seemed to be doing well in the theaters and wasn't Uncle Ray a famous sci-fi writer?— decided to hold out for the money they were sure was on the way, and quashed the original deal.

As of this writing, of course, Baker's *Fermata* has yet to be filmed, and the screenplay has gone through at least three versions. (A film in 2006, *Cashback*, did rip off that central conceit, but it lacked the grotesque seediness of Baker's novel, and pretty much everything from Lafferty's story.) And up through the actual sale of the estate to the Locus Foundation last year, "Six Fingers" was still the last and only high-dollar Hollywood option taken out on any of Lafferty's tales—which might have explained the willingness of the heirs to finally agree to the sale for $75,000 (with a provision for splitting the purse, should Tinseltown come calling in the future).

The odd thing in all this, of course (or *an* odd thing) is that the stoppage of time is likely the least original element in "Six Fingers of Time" (Robert Bloch's "The Hell-Bound Train" is only one of many tales around that time presenting similar temporal tricks). In Lafferty's telling, the time-manipulation and the juvenile pranks played by the protagonist are only the setup for a game played for much higher stakes than a peek or two in the women's locker room: the ability to greatly slow time is reserved for those who have, whether vestigially or fully-formed, six fingers on each hand,

and who belong to a different recension from the standard-issue man on the street.

Lafferty would use this background conspiracy more effectively in later works, especially *The Devil Is Dead* and the *Coscuin Chronicles*; here that history is compressed into the space of a novelette and made into a race against, not the time of the clock, but the span of one's life, as the hero must learn enough (across *many* disciplines—like Lafferty himself and many of his characters, this one's an autodidact) in the time he has to bring the conspiracy to light.

Thanks to its being in the public domain, "Six Fingers of Time" is the first Lafferty story many new readers encounter, though it is not an ideal starting point. It has all the horror of a great Lafferty work, but very little of the humor; the coexistence of the two is what marks him at his peak. Yet it is undeniably a story that leaves an impression: many among the non-devoted remember it with a chill, along with its implications of a global and likely cosmic conspiracy of extradigital individuals to maintain their immortality and amusement at the expense of all others on earth. Hell, even the number six itself is charged with a certain spookiness, a "wrongness" not in the least diminished by the thought that it divides neatly into all measurements of time.

The end of the tale is ambiguous: nearing the great vision of the conspiracy's extent and the transmission of that vision to the public, the prematurely aged protagonist dies in his sleep, and his adversaries sedately rejoice. For a decade such appeared to be the fate of Lafferty's own vision—until the sale of his estate to Locus gave instead a reason for all of his fans and supporters to rejoice. Let there be nothing sedate about it! But let us also remember that there remains much work to be done.

Finished December 1959. Published in If, ed. H.L. Gold, September 1960. Collected in Nine Hundred Grandmothers, New York: Ace Books, 1970.

Andrew Ferguson is a Ph.D candidate at the University of Virginia. He wrote on Lafferty for his MA thesis in Science Fiction Studies at the University of Liverpool, and is now building on this work for a biography in the University of Illinois' Modern Masters of Science Fiction series. His blog, "Continued on Next Rock," is at ralafferty.tumblr.com.

THE SIX FINGERS OF TIME
- a review by Kevin A. Cheek

*H*e began by breaking things that morning.

Bill Hader, in his much appreciated NYT article mentioned the first line of "The Six Fingers of Time" as an example of how engaging Lafferty Lunacy is. But in a way, what we have here is Lafferty in classic SF mode. This appears to be a simple story with a simple—almost Twilight-Zone-like twist at the end. Except that it isn't.

On one level, it is a very easy story, told in a prose style that is much more straightforward than some of Lafferty's more ebulliently effervescent efforts. The story proceeds and we keep guessing about 1/2 step ahead of the main character, but Lafferty still manages to surprise and delight us at the end. If that were all there is to this story, it would be a very good story.

But there is much more to the story. On another level, it is a story about ultimate temptation and choices. It asks if a man, Charles Vincent, the protagonist, is moral enough to choose faith and humanity when offered a chance to be a lord of time—to live a life as long as his mortal soul's and to therefore have power over time and fate—if only he'll choose to ally with certain powers that "smell of the pit". Ultimately Vincent chooses to reject the shadowy and perhaps demonic forces and to wrest that power from them for humanity. It is a valiant if doomed effort. On this level, it still uses the SF trope of the one clever man pitted against an organized army that holds all the cards in its hand. In the standard version of that story line, the one clever man succeeds, but in Lafferty's story, the mysterious enemy continues to hold all the cards—beginning, middle, and end.

And on yet another level, it is the story of the forces that beset humanity. He hints at a conspiracy, far older than Humanity and far older than Humanity's current bargain with God in the Garden. This conspiracy lives on in vestigial form in modern Humanity—in this story taking the form of a mutation for six fingers on the hand. The members of this conspiracy claim that by right of prior occupation, they are exempt from such concepts as good and evil, salvation and damnation. The idea of a prehistoric, genetic conspiracy of an older race against mankind is the nexus of *The Devil is Dead* and *Fourth Mansions*. It seems to underlie a large portion of Lafferty's work, with the message that as humans we are beset, but we may just have the creativity, energy, and faith to overcome and eliminate these conspiracies.

"The Six Fingers of Time" was an early work of Lafferty's, finished in 1959, and first published in 1960. Consider the state of Science Fiction in 1960. Standard "Golden Age" storytelling was still dominant. Shows like *The Twilight Zone* were just getting started with admittedly very good writing and perhaps a sting in the tail. And here Lafferty gives us a story that is one on level a fun, easy story about a man learning a trick and being tricked in the end. On another level it is a battle within a human soul between temptation and ethics; on another, it is the introduction to an ongoing examination of the forces that metaphorically beset us in our journey toward spiritual evolution.

So the opening line of the story, I think applies very well to Lafferty's writing in general: "He began by breaking things."

THE SIX FINGERS OF TIME
by R. A. Lafferty

Originally published in the September 1960 issue of
If. This text was derived from the Project Gutenberg
eText (http://www.gutenberg.org/ebooks/31663)

THE

SIX

FINGERS

OF

TIME

Time is money.

Time heals all wounds.

Given time, anything is possible.

And now he had all the time in

the world!

By R. A. LAFFERTY

Illustrated by GAUGHAN

H<small>E</small> BEGAN by breaking things that morning. He broke the glass of water on his night stand. He knocked it crazily against the opposite wall and shattered it. Yet it shattered slowly. This would have surprised him if he had been fully awake, for he had only reached out sleepily for it.

Nor had he wakened regularly to his alarm; he had wakened to a weird, slow, low booming, yet the clock said six, time for the alarm. And the low boom, when it came again, seemed to come from the clock.

He reached out and touched it gently, but it floated off the stand at his touch and bounced around slowly on the floor. And when he picked it up again it had stopped, nor would shaking start it.

He checked the electric clock in the kitchen. This also said six o'clock, but the sweep hand did not move. In his living room the radio clock said six, but the second hand seemed stationary.

"But the lights in both rooms work," said Vincent. "How are the clocks stopped? Are they on a separate circuit?"

He went back to his bedroom and got his wristwatch. It also said six; and its sweep hand did not sweep.

"Now this could get silly. What is it that would stop both mechanical and electrical clocks?"

He went to the window and looked out at the clock on the Mutual Insurance Building. It said six o'clock, and the second hand did not move.

"Well, it is possible that the confusion is not limited to myself. I once heard the fanciful theory that a cold shower will clear the mind. For me it never has, but I will try it. I can always use cleanliness for an excuse."

The shower didn't work. Yes, it did: the water came now, but not like water; like very slow syrup that hung in the air. He reached up to touch it there hanging down and stretching. And it shattered like glass when he touched it and drifted in fantastic slow globs across the room. But it had the feel of water, wet and pleasantly cool. And in a quarter of a minute or so it was down over his shoulders and back, and he luxuriated in it. He let it soak his head and it cleared his wits at once.

"There is not a thing wrong with me. I am fine. It is not my fault that the water is slow this morning and other things awry."

He reached for the towel and it tore to pieces in his hands like porous wet paper.

N OW he became very careful in the way he handled things. Slowly, tenderly, and deftly he took them so that they would not break. He shaved himself without mishap in spite of the slow water in the lavatory also.

Then he dressed himself with the greatest caution and cunning, breaking nothing except his shoe laces, a thing that is likely to happen at any time.

"If there is nothing the matter with me, then I will check and see if there is anything seriously wrong with the world. The dawn was fairly along when I looked out, as it should have been. Approximately twenty minutes have passed; it is a clear morning; the sun should now have hit the top several stories of the Insurance Building."

But it had not. It was a clear morning, but the dawn had not brightened at all in the twenty minutes. And that big clock still said six. It had not changed.

Yet it had changed, and he knew it with a queer feeling. He pictured it as it had been before. The hour and the minute hand had not moved noticeably. But the second hand had moved. It had moved a third of the dial.

So he pulled up a chair to the window and watched it. He realized that, though he could not see it move, yet it did make progress. He watched it for perhaps five minutes. It moved through a space of perhaps five seconds.

"Well, that is not my problem. It is that of the clock maker, either a terrestrial or a celestial one."

But he left his rooms without a good breakfast, and he left them very early. How did he know that it was early since there was something wrong with the time? Well, it was early at least according to the sun and according to the clocks, neither of which institutions seemed to be working properly.

He left without a good breakfast because the coffee would not make and the bacon would not fry. And in plain point of fact the fire would not heat. The gas flame came from the pilot light like a slowly spreading stream or an unfolding flower. Then it burned far too steadily. The skillet remained cold when placed over it; nor would water even heat. It had taken at least five minutes to get the water out of the faucet in the first place.

He ate a few pieces of leftover bread and some scraps of meat.

In the street there was no motion, no real motion. A truck, first seeming at rest, moved very slowly. There was no gear in which it could move so slowly. And there was a taxi which crept along, but Charles Vincent had to look at it carefully for some time to be sure that it was in motion. Then he received a shock. He realized by the early morning light that the driver of it was dead. Dead with his eyes wide open!

Slowly as it was going, and by whatever means it was moving, it should really be stopped. He walked over to it, opened the door, and pulled on the brake. Then he looked into the eyes of the dead man. Was he really dead? It was hard to be sure. He felt warm. But, even as Vincent looked, the eyes of the dead man had begun to close. And close they did and open again in a matter of about twenty seconds.

THIS was weird. The slowly closing and opening eyes sent a chill through Vincent. And the dead man had begun to lean forward in his seat. Vincent put a hand in the middle of the man's chest to hold him upright, but he found the forward pressure as relentless as it was slow. He was unable to keep the dead man up.

So he let him go, watching curiously; and in a few seconds the driver's face was against the wheel. But it was almost as if it had no intention of stopping there. It pressed into the wheel with dogged force. He would surely break his face. Vincent took several holds on the dead man and counteracted the pressure somewhat. Yet the face was being damaged, and if things were normal, blood would have flowed.

The man had been dead so long however, that (though he was still warm) his blood must have congealed, for it was fully two minutes before it began to ooze.

"Whatever I have done, I have done enough damage," said Vincent. "And, in whatever nightmare I am in, I am likely to do further harm if I meddle more. I had better leave it alone."

He walked on down the morning street. Yet whatever vehicles he saw were moving with an incredible slowness, as though driven by some fantastic gear reduction. And there were people here and there frozen solid. It was a chilly morning, but it was not that cold. They were immobile in positions of motion, as though they were playing the children's game of Statues.

"How is it," said Charles Vincent, "that this young girl (who I believe works across the street from us) should have died standing up and in full stride? But, no. She is not dead. Or, if so, she died with a very alert expression. And—oh, my God, she's doing it too!"

For he realized that the eyes of the girl were closing, and in the space of no more than a quarter of a second they had completed their cycle and were open again. Also, and this was even stranger, she had moved, moved forward in full stride. He would have timed her if he could, but how could he when all the clocks were crazy? Yet she must have been taking about two steps a minute.

He went into the cafeteria. The early morning crowd that he had often watched through the windows was there. The girl who made flapjacks in the window had just flipped one and it hung in the air. Then it floated over as if caught by a slight breeze, and sank slowly down as if settling in water.

The breakfasters, like the people in the street, were all dead in this new way, moving with almost imperceptible motion. And all had apparently died in the act of drinking coffee, eating eggs, or munching toast. And if there were only time enough, there was even a chance that they would get the drinking, eating, and munching done with, for there was the shadow of movement in them all.

The cashier had the register drawer open and money in her hand, and the hand of the customer was outstretched for it. In time, somewhere in the new leisurely time, the hands would come together and the change be given. And so it happened. It may have been a minute and a half, or two minutes, or two and a half. It is always hard to judge time, and now it had become all but impossible.

"I am still hungry," said Charles Vincent, "but it would be foolhardy to wait for service here. Should I help myself? They will not mind if they are dead. And if they are not dead, in any case it seems that I am invisible to them."

H E WOLFED several rolls. He opened a bottle of milk and held it upside down over his glass while he ate another roll. Liquids had all become perversely slow.

But he felt better for his erratic breakfast. He would have paid for it, but how?

He left the cafeteria and walked about the town as it seemed still to be quite early, though one could depend on neither sun nor clock for the time any more. The traffic lights were unchanging. He sat for a long time in a little park and watched the town and the big clock in the Commerce Building tower; but like all the clocks it was either stopped or the hand would creep too slowly to be seen.

It must have been just about an hour till the traffic lights changed, but change they did at last. By picking a point on the building across the street and watching what moved past it, he found that the traffic did indeed move. In a minute or so, the entire length of a car would pass the given point.

He had, he recalled, been very far behind in his work and it had been worrying him. He decided to go to the office, early as it was or seemed to be.

He let himself in. Nobody else was there. He resolved not to look at the clock and to be very careful of the way he handled all objects because of his new propensity for breaking things. This considered, all seemed normal there. He had said the day before that he could hardly catch up on his work if he put in two days solid. He now resolved at least to work steadily until something happened, whatever it was.

For hour after hour he worked on his tabulations and reports. Nobody else had arrived. Could something be wrong? Certainly something was wrong. But this was not a holiday. That was not it.

Just how long can a stubborn and mystified man plug away at his task? It was hour after hour after hour. He did not become hungry nor particularly tired. And he did get through a lot of work.

"It must be half done. However it has happened, I have caught up on at least a day's work. I will keep on."

He must have continued silently for another eight or ten hours.

He was caught up completely on his back work.

"Well, to some extent I can work into the future. I can head up and carry over. I can put in everything but the figures of the field reports."

And he did so.

"It will be hard to bury me in work again. I could almost coast for a day. I don't even know what day it is, but I must have worked twenty hours straight through and nobody has arrived. Perhaps nobody ever will arrive. If they are moving with the speed of the people in the nightmare outside, it is no wonder they have not arrived."

He put his head down on his arms on the desk. The last thing he saw before he closed his eyes was the misshapen left thumb that he had always tried to conceal a little by the way he handled his hands.

"At least I know that I am still myself. I'd know myself anywhere by that."

Then he went to sleep at his desk.

JENNY came in with a quick click-click-click of high heels, and he wakened to the noise.

"What are you doing dozing at your desk, Mr. Vincent? Have you been here all night?"

"I don't know, Jenny. Honestly I don't."

"I was only teasing. Sometimes when I get here a little early I take a catnap myself."

The clock said six minutes till eight and the second hand was sweeping normally. Time had returned to the world. Or to him. But had all that early morning of his been a dream? Then it had been a very efficient dream. He had accomplished work that he could hardly have done in two days. And it was the same day that it was supposed to be.

He went to the water fountain. The water now behaved normally. He went to the window. The traffic was behaving as it should. Though sometimes slow and sometimes snarled, yet it was in the pace of the regular world.

The other workers arrived. They were not balls of fire, but neither was it necessary to observe them for several minutes to be sure they weren't dead.

"It did have its advantages," Charles Vincent said. "I would be afraid to live with it permanently, but it would be handy to go into for a few minutes a day and accomplish the business of hours. I may be a case for the doctor. But just how would I go about telling a doctor what was bothering me?"

Now it had surely been less than two hours from his first rising till the time that he wakened to the noise of Jenny from his second sleep. And how long that second sleep had been, or in which time enclave, he had no idea. But how account for it all? He had spent a long while in his own rooms, much longer than ordinary in his confusion. He had walked the city mile after mile in his puzzlement. And he had sat in the little park for hours and studied the situation. And he had worked at his own desk for an outlandish long time.

Well, he would go to the doctor. A man is obliged to refrain from making a fool of himself to the world at large, but to his own lawyer, his priest, or his doctor he will sometimes have to come as a fool. By their callings they are restrained from scoffing openly.

Dr. Mason was not particularly a friend. Charles Vincent realized with some unease that he did not have any particular friends, only acquaintances and associates. It was as though he were of a species slightly apart from his fellows. He wished now a little that he had a particular friend.

But Dr. Mason was an acquaintance of some years, had the reputation of being a good doctor, and besides Vincent had now arrived at his office and been shown in. He would either have to— well, that was as good a beginning as any.

"Doctor, I am in a predicament. I will either have to invent some symptoms to account for my visit here, or make an excuse and bolt, or tell you what is bothering me, even though you will think I am a new sort of idiot."

"Vincent, every day people invent symptoms to cover their visits here, and I know that they have lost their nerve about the real reason for coming. And every day people do make excuses and bolt. But experience tells me that I will get a larger fee if you tackle the third alternative. And, Vincent, there is no new sort of idiot."

V INCENT said, "It may not sound so silly if I tell it quickly. I awoke this morning to some very puzzling incidents. It seemed that time itself had stopped, or that the whole world had gone into super-slow motion. The water would neither flow nor boil, and fire would not heat food. The clocks, which I first believed had stopped, crept along at perhaps a minute an hour. The people I met in the streets appeared dead, frozen in lifelike attitudes. And it was only by watching them for a very long time that I perceived that they did indeed have motion. One car I saw creeping slower than the most backward snail, and a dead man at the wheel of it. I went to it, opened the door, and put on the brake. I realized after a time that the man was not dead. But he bent forward and broke his face on the steering wheel. It must have taken a full minute for his head to travel no more than ten inches, yet I was unable to prevent his hitting the wheel. I then did other bizarre things in a world that had died on its feet. I walked many miles through the city, and then I sat for hours in the park. I went to the office and let myself in. I accomplished work that must have taken me twenty hours. I then took a nap at my desk. When I awoke on the arrival of the others, it was six minutes to eight in the morning of the same day, today. Not two hours had passed from my rising, and time was back to normal. But the things that happened in that time that could never be compressed into two hours."

"One question first, Vincent. Did you actually accomplish the work of many hours?"

"I did. It was done, and done in that time. It did not become undone on the return of time to normal."

"A second question. Had you been worried about your work, about being behind?"

"Yes. Emphatically."

"Then here is one explanation. You retired last night. But very shortly afterward you arose in a state of somnambulism. There are facets of sleepwalking which we do not at all understand. The time-out-of-focus interludes were parts of a walking dream of yours. You dressed and went to your office and worked all night. It is possible to do routine tasks in a somnambulistic state rapidly and even feverishly, with an intense concentration—to perform prodigies. You may have fallen into a normal sleep there when you had finished, or you may have been awakened directly from your somnambulistic trance on the arrival of your co-workers. There, that is a plausible and workable explanation. In the case of an apparently bizarre happening, it is always well to have a rational explanation to fall back on. They will usually satisfy a patient and put his mind at rest. But often they do not satisfy me."

"Your explanation very nearly satisfies me, Dr. Mason, and it does put my mind considerably at rest. I am sure that in a short while I will be able to accept it completely. But why does it not satisfy you?"

"One reason is a man I treated early this morning. He had his face smashed, and he had seen—or almost seen—a ghost: a ghost of incredible swiftness that was more sensed than seen. The ghost opened the door of his car while it was going at full speed, jerked on the brake, and caused him to crack his head. This man was dazed and had a slight concussion. I have convinced him that he did not see any ghost at all, that he must have dozed at the wheel and run into something. As I say, I am harder to convince than my patients. But it may have been coincidence."

"I hope so. But you also seem to have another reservation."

"After quite a few years in practice, I seldom see or hear anything new. Twice before I have been told a happening or a dream on the line of what you experienced."

"Did you convince your patients that it was only a dream?"

"I did. Both of them. That is, I convinced them the first few times it happened to them."

"Were they satisfied?"

"At first. Later, not entirely. But they both died within a year of their first coming to me."

"Nothing violent, I hope."

"Both had the gentlest deaths. That of senility extreme."

"Oh. Well, I'm too young for that."

"I would like you to come back in a month or so."

"I will, if the delusion or the dream returns. Or if I do not feel well."

After this Charles Vincent began to forget about the incident. He only recalled it with humor sometimes when again he was behind in his work.

"Well, if it gets bad enough I may do another sleepwalking act and catch up. But if there is another aspect of time and I could enter it at will, it might often be handy."

CHARLES VINCENT never saw his face at all. It is very dark in some of those clubs and the Coq Bleu is like the inside of a tomb. He went to the clubs only about once a month, sometimes after a show when he did not want to go home to bed, sometimes when he was just plain restless.

Citizens of the more fortunate states may not know of the mysteries of the clubs. In Vincent's the only bars are beer bars, and only in the clubs can a person get a drink, and only members are admitted. It is true that even such a small club as the Coq Bleu had thirty thousand members, and at a dollar a year that is a nice sideline. The little numbered membership cards cost a penny each for the printing, and the member wrote in his own name. But he had to have a card—or a dollar for a card—to gain admittance.

But there could be no entertainments in the clubs. There was nothing there but the little bar room in the near darkness.

The man was there, and then he was not, and then he was there again. And always where he sat it was too dark to see his face.

"I wonder," he said to Vincent (or to the bar at large, though there were no other customers and the bartender was asleep), "I wonder if you have ever read Zurbarin on the Relationship of Extradigitalism to Genius?"

"I have never heard of the work nor of the man," said Vincent. "I doubt if either exists."

"I am Zurbarin," said the man.

Vincent hid his misshapen left thumb. Yet it could not have

been noticed in that light, and he must have been crazy to believe there was any connection between it and the man's remark. It was not truly a double thumb. He was not an extradigital, nor was he a genius.

"I refuse to become interested in you," said Vincent. "I am on the verge of leaving. I dislike waking the bartender, but I did want another drink."

"Sooner done than said."

"What is?"

"Your glass is full."

"It is? So it is. Is it a trick?"

"Trick is the name for anything either too frivolous or too mystifying for us to comprehend. But on one long early morning of a month ago, you also could have done the trick, and nearly as well."

"Could I have? How would you know about my long early morning—assuming there to have been such?"

"I watched you for a while. Few others have the equipment to watch you with when you're in the aspect."

S O THEY were silent for some time, and Vincent watched the clock and was ready to go.

"I wonder," said the man in the dark, "if you have read

Schimmelpenninck on the Sexagintal and the Duodecimal in the Chaldee Mysteries?"

"I have not and I doubt if anyone else has. I would guess that you are also Schimmelpenninck and that you have just made up the name on the spur of the moment."

"I am Schimm, it is true, but I made up the name on the spur of a moment many years ago."

"I am a little bored with you," said Vincent, "but I would appreciate it if you'd do your glass-filling trick once more."

"I have just done so. And you are not bored; you are frightened."

"Of what?" asked Vincent, whose glass was in fact full again.

"Of reentering a dread that you are not sure was a dream. But there are advantages to being both invisible and inaudible."

"Can you be invisible?"

"Was I not when I went behind the bar just now and fixed you a drink?"

"How?"

"A man in full stride goes at the rate of about five miles an hour. Multiply that by sixty, which is the number of time. When I leave my stool and go behind the bar, I go and return at the rate of three hundred miles an hour. So I am invisible to you, particularly if I move while you blink."

"One thing does not match. You might have got around there and back, but you could not have poured."

"Shall I say that mastery over liquids is not given to beginners? But for us there are many ways to outwit the slowness of matter."

"I believe that you are a hoaxer. Do you know Dr. Mason?"

"I know that you went to see him. I know of his futile attempts to penetrate a certain mystery. But I have not talked to him of you."

"I still believe that you are a phony. Could you put me back into the state of my dream of a month ago?"

"It was not a dream. But I could put you again into that state."

"Prove it."

"Watch the clock. Do you believe that I can point my finger at it and stop it for you? It is already stopped for me."

"No, I don't believe it. Yes, I guess I have to, since I see that you have just done it. But it may be another trick. I don't know where the clock is plugged in."

"Neither do I. Come to the door. Look at every clock you can see. Are they not all stopped?"

"Yes. Maybe the power has gone off all over town."

"You know it has not. There are still lighted windows in those buildings, though it is quite late."

"Why are you playing with me? I am neither on the inside nor the outside. Either tell me the secret or say that you will not tell me."

"The secret isn't a simple one. It can only be arrived at after all philosophy and learning have been assimilated."

"One man cannot arrive at that in one lifetime."

"Not in an ordinary lifetime. But the secret of the secret (if I may put it that way) is that one must use part of it as a tool in learning. You could not learn all in one lifetime, but by being permitted the first step—to be able to read, say, sixty books in the time it took you to read one, to pause for a minute in thought and use up only one second, to get a day's work accomplished in eight minutes and so have time for other things—by such ways one may make a beginning. I will warn you, though. Even for the most intelligent, it is a race."

"A race? What race?"

"It is a race between success, which is life, and failure, which is death."

"Let's skip the melodrama. How do I get into the state and out of it?"

"Oh, that is simple, so easy that it seems like a gadget. Here are two diagrams I will draw. Note them carefully. This first, envision it in your mind and you are in the state. Now this second one, envision, and you are out of it."

"That easy?"

"That deceptively easy. The trick is to learn why it works—if you want to succeed, meaning to live."

So Charles Vincent left him and went home, walking the mile in a little less than fifteen normal seconds. But he still had not seen the face of the man.

THERE are advantages intellectual, monetary, and amorous in being able to enter the accelerated state at will. It is a fox game. One must be careful not to be caught at it, nor to break or harm that which is in the normal state.

Vincent could always find eight or ten minutes unobserved to accomplish the day's work. And a fifteen-minute coffee break could turn into a fifteen-hour romp around the town.

There was this boyish pleasure in becoming a ghost: to appear and stand motionless in front of an onrushing train and to cause the scream of the whistle, and to be in no danger, being able to move five or ten times as fast as the train; to enter and to sit suddenly in the middle of a select group and see them stare, and then disappear from the middle of them; to interfere in sports and games, entering a prize ring and tripping, hampering, or slugging the unliked fighter; to blue-shot down the hockey ice, skating at fifteen hundred miles an hour and scoring dozens of goals at either end while the people only know that something odd is happening.

There was pleasure in being able to shatter windows by chanting little songs, for the voice (when in the state) will be to the world at sixty times its regular pitch, though normal to oneself. And for this reason also he was inaudible to others.

There was fun in petty thieving and tricks. He would take a

wallet from a man's pocket and be two blocks away when the victim turned at the feel. He would come back and stuff it into the man's mouth as he bleated to a policeman.

He would come into the home of a lady writing a letter, snatch up the paper and write three lines and vanish before the scream got out of her throat.

He would take food off forks, put baby turtles and live fish into bowls of soup between spoonfuls of the eater.

He would lash the hands of handshakers tightly together with stout cord. He unzippered persons of both sexes when they were at their most pompous. He changed cards from one player's hand to another's. He removed golf balls from tees during the backswing and left notes written large "YOU MISSED ME" pinned to the ground with the tee.

Or he shaved mustaches and heads. Returning repeatedly to one woman he disliked, he gradually clipped her bald and finally gilded her pate.

With tellers counting their money, he interfered outrageously and enriched himself. He snipped cigarettes in two with a scissors and blew out matches, so that one frustrated man broke down and cried at his inability to get a light.

He removed the weapons from the holsters of policemen and put cap pistols and water guns in their places. He unclipped the leashes of dogs and substituted little toy dogs rolling on wheels.

He put frogs in water glasses and left lighted firecrackers on bridge tables.

He reset wrist watches on wrists, and played pranks in men's rooms.

"I was always a boy at heart," said Charles Vincent.

A LSO during those first few days of the controlled new state, he established himself materially, acquiring wealth by devious ways, and opening bank accounts in various cities under various names, against a time of possible need.

Nor did he ever feel any shame for the tricks he played on unaccelerated humanity. For the people, when he was in the state, were as statues to him, hardly living, barely moving, unseeing, unhearing. And it is no shame to show disrespect to such comical statues.

And also, and again because he was a boy at heart, he had fun with the girls.

"I am one mass of black and blue marks," said Jenny one day. "My lips are sore and my front teeth feel loosened. I don't know what in the world is the matter with me."

Yet he had not meant to bruise or harm her. He was rather fond of her and he resolved to be much more careful. Yet it was fun, when he was in the state and invisible to her because of his speed, to kiss her here and there in out-of-the-way places. She made a nice statue and it was good sport. And there were others.

"You look older," said one of his co-workers one day. "Are you taking care of yourself? Are you worried?"

"I am not," said Vincent. "I never felt better or happier in my life."

But now there was time for so many things—time, in fact, for everything. There was no reason why he could not master anything in the world, when he could take off for fifteen minutes and gain fifteen hours. Vincent was a rapid but careful reader. He could now read from a hundred and twenty to two hundred books in an evening and night; and he slept in the accelerated state and could get a full night's sleep in eight minutes.

He first acquired a knowledge of languages. A quite extensive reading knowledge of a language can be acquired in three hundred hours world time, or three hundred minutes (five hours) accelerated time. And if one takes the tongues in order, from the most familiar to the most remote, there is no real difficulty. He acquired fifty for a starter, and could always add any other any evening that he found he had a need for it. And at the same time he began to assemble and consolidate knowledge. Of literature, properly speaking, there are no more than ten thousand books that are really worth reading and falling in love with. These were gone through with high pleasure, and two or three thousand of them were important enough to be reserved for future rereading.

History, however, is very uneven; and it is necessary to read texts and sources that for form are not worth reading. And the same with philosophy. Mathematics and science, pure or physical, could not, of course, be covered with the same speed. Yet, with time available, all could be mastered. There is no concept ever expressed by any human mind that cannot be comprehended by any other normal human mind, if time is available and it is taken in the proper order and context and with the proper preparatory work.

And often, and now more often, Vincent felt that he was

touching the fingers of the secret; and always, when he came near it, it had a little bit the smell of the pit.

For he had pegged out all the main points of the history of man; or rather most of the tenable, or at least possible, theories of the history of man. It was hard to hold the main line of it, that double road of rationality and revelation that should lead always to a fuller and fuller development (not the fetish of progress, that toy word used only by toy people), to an unfolding and growth and perfectibility.

But the main line was often obscure and all but obliterated, and traced through fog and miasma. He had accepted the Fall of Man and the Redemption as the cardinal points of history. But he understood now that neither happened only once, that both were of constant occurrence; that there was a hand reaching up from that old pit with its shadow over man. And he had come to picture that hand in his dreams (for his dreams were especially vivid when in the state) as a six-digited monster reaching out. He began to realize that the thing he was caught in was dangerous and deadly.

Very dangerous.

Very deadly.

One of the weird books that he often returned to and which continually puzzled him was the Relationship of Extradigitalism to Genius, written by the man whose face he had never seen, in one of his manifestations.

It promised more than it delivered, and it intimated more than it said. Its theory was tedious and tenuous, bolstered with undigested mountains of doubtful data. It left him unconvinced that persons of genius (even if it could be agreed who or what they were) had often the oddity of extra fingers and toes, or the vestiges of them. And it puzzled him what possible difference it could make.

Y ET there were hints here of a Corsican who commonly kept a hand hidden, or an earlier and more bizarre commander who wore always a mailed glove, of another man with a glove between the two; hints that the multiplex-adept, Leonardo himself, who sometimes drew the hands of men and often those of monsters with six fingers, may himself have had the touch. There was a comment of Caesar, not conclusive, to the same effect. It is known that Alexander had a minor peculiarity; it is not known what it was; this man made it seem that this was it. And it was averred of Gregory and Augustine, of Benedict and Albert and Acquinas. Yet a man with a deformity could not enter the priesthood; if they had it, it must have been in vestigial form.

There were cases for Charles Magnut and Mahmud, for Saladin the Horseman and for Akhnaton the King; for Homer (a Seleuciad-Greek statuette shows him with six fingers strumming an unidentified instrument while reciting); for Pythagoras, for Buonarroti, Santi, Theotokopolous, van Rijn, Robusti.

Zurbarin catalogued eight thousand names. He maintained that they were geniuses. And that they were extradigitals.

Charles Vincent grinned and looked down at his misshapen or double thumb.

"At least I am in good though monotonous company. But what in the name of triple time is he driving at?"

And it was not long afterward that Vincent was examining cuneiform tablets in the State Museum. These were a broken and not continuous series on the theory of numbers, tolerably legible to the now encyclopedic Charles Vincent. And the series read in part:

"On the divergence of the basis itself and the confusion caused —for it is five, or it is six, or ten or twelve, or sixty or a hundred, or three hundred and sixty or the double hundred, the thousand. The reason, not clearly understood by the people, is that Six and the Dozen are first, and Sixty is a compromise in condescending to the people. For the five, the ten are late, and are no older than the people themselves. It is said, and credited, that people began to count by fives and tens from the number of fingers on their hands. But before the people the—by the reason that they had—counted by sixes and twelves. But Sixty is the number of time, divisible by both, for both must live together in time, though not on the same plane of time—" Much of the rest was scattered. And it was while trying to set the hundreds of unordered clay tablets in proper sequence that Charles Vincent created the legend of the ghost in the museum.

For he spent his multi-hundred-hour nights there studying and classifying. Naturally he could not work without light, and naturally he could be seen when he sat still at his studies. But as the slow-moving guards attempted to close in on him, he would move to avoid them, and his speed made him invisible to them. They were a nuisance and had to be discouraged. He belabored them soundly and they became less eager to try to capture him.

His only fear was that they would some time try to shoot him to see if he were ghost or human. He could avoid a seen shot, which would come at no more than two and a half times his own greatest speed. But an unperceived shot could penetrate dangerously, even fatally, before he twisted away from it.

He had fathered legends of other ghosts, that of the Central

Library, that of University Library, that of the John Charles Underwood Jr. Technical Library. This plurality of ghosts tended to cancel out each other and bring believers into ridicule. Even those who had seen him as a ghost did not admit that they believed in the ghosts.

H E WENT back to Dr. Mason for his monthly checkup.

"You look terrible," said the Doctor. "Whatever it is, you have changed. If you can afford it, you should take a long rest."

"I have the means," said Charles Vincent, "and that is just what I will do. I'll take a rest for a year or two."

He had begun to begrudge the time that he must spend at the world's pace. From now on he was regarded as a recluse. He was silent and unsociable, for he found it a nuisance to come back to the common state to engage in conversation, and in his special state voices were too slow-pitched to intrude into his consciousness.

Except that of the man whose face he had never seen.

"You are making very tardy progress," said the man. Once more they were in a dark club. "Those who do not show more progress we cannot use. After all, you are only a vestigial. It is probable that you have very little of the ancient race in you. Fortunately those who do not show progress destroy themselves. You had not imagined that there were only two phases of time, had you?"

"Lately I have come to suspect that there are many more," said

Charles Vincent.

"And you understand that only one step cannot succeed?"

"I understand that the life I have been living is in direct violation of all that we know of the laws of mass, momentum, and acceleration, as well as those of conservation of energy, the potential of the human person, the moral compensation, the golden mean, and the capacity of human organs. I know that I cannot multiply energy and experience sixty times without a compensating increase of food intake, and yet I do it. I know that I cannot live on eight minutes' sleep in twenty-four hours, but I do that also. I know that I cannot reasonably crowd four thousand years of experience into one lifetime, yet unreasonably I do not see what will prevent it. But you say I will destroy myself."

"Those who take only the first step destroy themselves."

"And how does one take the second step?"

"At the proper moment you will be given the choice."

"I have the most uncanny feeling that I will refuse the choice."

"From present indications, you will refuse it. You are fastidious."

"You have a smell about you, Old Man without a face. I know now what it is. It is the smell of the pit."

"Are you so slow to learn that?"

"It is the mud from the pit, the same from which the clay tablets were formed, from the old land between the rivers. I've dreamed of the six-fingered hand reaching up from the pit and overshadowing us all. And I have read: 'The people first counted by fives and tens from the number of fingers on their hands. But before the people—for the reason that they had—counted by sixes and twelves.' But time has left blanks in those tablets."

"Yes, time in one of its manifestations has deftly and with a purpose left those blanks."

"I cannot discover the name of the thing that goes in one of those blanks. Can you?"

"I am part of the name that goes into one of those blanks."

"And you are the man without a face. But why is it that you overshadow and control people? And to what purpose?"

"It will be long before you know those answers."

"When the choice comes to me, it will bear very careful weighing."

AFTER that a chill descended on the life of Charles Vincent, for all that he still possessed his exceptional powers. And he seldom now indulged in pranks.

Except for Jennifer Parkey.

It was unusual that he should be drawn to her. He knew her only slightly in the common world and she was at least fifteen years his senior. But now she appealed to him for her youthful qualities, and all his pranks with her were gentle ones.

For one thing this spinster did not frighten, nor did she begin locking her doors, never having bothered about such things before. He would come behind her and stroke her hair, and she would speak out calmly with that sort of quickening in her voice: "Who are you? Why won't you let me see you? You are a friend, aren't you? Are you a man, or are you something else? If you can caress me, why can't you talk to me? Please let me see you. I promise that I won't hurt you."

It was as though she could not imagine that anything strange would hurt her. Or again when he hugged her or kissed her on the nape, she would call: "You must be a little boy, or very like a little boy, whoever you are. You are good not to break my things when you move about. Come here and let me hold you."

It is only very good people who have no fear at all of the unknown.

When Vincent met Jennifer in the regular world, as he more often now found occasion to do, she looked at him appraisingly, as though she guessed some sort of connection.

She said one day: "I know it is an impolite thing to say, but you do not look well at all. Have you been to a doctor?"

"Several times. But I think it is my doctor who should go to a doctor. He was always given to peculiar remarks, but now he is becoming a little unsettled."

"If I were your doctor, I believe I would also become a little unsettled. But you should find out what is wrong. You look terrible."

He did not look terrible. He had lost his hair, it is true, but many men lose their hair by thirty, though not perhaps as suddenly as he had. He thought of attributing it to the air resistance. After all, when he was in the state he did stride at some three hundred miles an hour. And enough of that is likely to blow the hair right off your head. And might that not also be the reason for his worsened complexion and the tireder look that appeared in his eyes? But he knew that this was nonsense. He felt no more air pressure when in his accelerated state than when in the normal one.

He had received his summons. He chose not to answer it. He did not want to be presented with the choice; he had no wish to be one with those of the pit. But he had no intention of giving up the great advantage which he now held over nature.

"I will have it both ways," he said. "I am already a contradiction and an impossibility. The proverb was only the early statement of the law of moral compensation: 'You can't take more out of a basket than it holds.' But for a long time I have been in violation of the laws and balances. 'There is no road without a turning,' 'Those who dance will have to pay the fiddler,' 'Everything that goes up comes down,' But are proverbs really universal laws? Certainly. A sound proverb has the force of universal law; it is but another statement of it. But I have contradicted the universal laws. It remains to be seen whether I have contradicted them with impunity. 'Every action has its reaction.' If I refuse to deal with them, I will provoke a strong reaction. The man without a face said that it was always a race between full knowing and destruction. Very well, I will race them for it."

THEY began to persecute him then. He knew that they were in a state as accelerated from his as his was from the normal. To them he was the almost motionless statue, hardly to be told from a dead man. To him they were by their speed both invisible and inaudible. They hurt him and haunted him. But still he would not answer the summons.

When the meeting took place, it was they who had to come to him, and they materialized there in his room, men without faces.

"The choice," said one. "You force us to be so clumsy as to have to voice it."

"I will have no part of you. You all smell of the pit, of that old mud of the cuneiforms of the land between the rivers, of the people who were before the people."

"It has endured a long time, and we consider it as enduring forever. But the Garden which was in the neighborhood—do you know how long the Garden lasted?"

"I don't know."

"That all happened in a single day, and before nightfall they were outside. You want to throw in with something more permanent, don't you."

"No. I don't believe I do."

"What have you to lose?"

"Only my hope of eternity."

"But you don't believe in that. No man has ever really believed in eternity."

"No man has ever either entirely believed or disbelieved in it," said Charles Vincent.

"At least it cannot be proved," said one of the faceless men. "Nothing is proved until it is over with. And in this case, if it is ever over with, then it is disproved. And all that time would one not be tempted to wonder, 'What if, after all, it ends in the next minute?'"

"I imagine that if we survive the flesh we will receive some sort of surety," said Vincent.

"But you are not sure either of such surviving or receiving. Now *we* have a very close approximation of eternity. When time is multiplied by itself, and that repeated again and again, does that not approximate eternity?"

"I don't believe it does. But I will not be of you. One of you has said that I am too fastidious. So now will you say that you'll destroy me?"

"No. We will only let you be destroyed. By yourself, you cannot win the race with destruction."

After that Charles Vincent somehow felt more mature. He knew he was not really meant to be a six-fingered thing of the pit. He knew that in some way he would have to pay for every minute and hour that he had gained. But what he had gained he would use to the fullest. And whatever could be accomplished by sheer acquisition of human knowledge, he would try to accomplish.

And he now startled Dr. Mason by the medical knowledge he had picked up, the while the doctor amused him by the concern he showed for Vincent. For he felt fine. He was perhaps not as active as he had been, but that was only because he had become dubious of aimless activity. He was still the ghost of the libraries and museums, but was puzzled that the published reports intimated that an old ghost had replaced a young one.

He NOW paid his mystic visits to Jennifer Parkey less often. For he was always dismayed to hear her exclaim to him in his ghostly form: "Your touch is so changed. You poor thing! Is there anything at all I can do to help you?"

He decided that somehow she was too immature to understand him, though he was still fond of her. He transferred his affections to Mrs. Milly Maltby, a widow at least thirty years his senior. Yet here it was a sort of girlishness in her that appealed to him. She was a woman of sharp wit and real affection, and she also accepted his visitations without fear, following a little initial panic.

They played games, writing games, for they communicated by writing. She would scribble a line, then hold the paper up in the air whence he would cause it to vanish into his sphere. He would return it in half a minute, or half a second by her time, with his retort. He had the advantage of her in time with greatly more opportunity to think up responses, but she had the advantage over him in natural wit and was hard to top.

They also played checkers, and he often had to retire apart and read a chapter of a book on the art between moves, and even so she often beat him; for native talent is likely to be a match for accumulated lore and codified procedure.

But to Milly also he was unfaithful in his fashion, being now interested (he no longer became enamored or entranced) in a Mrs. Roberts, a great-grandmother who was his elder by at least fifty years. He had read all the data extant on the attraction of the old for the young, but he still could not explain his successive attachments. He decided that these three examples were enough to establish a universal law: that a woman is simply not afraid of a ghost, though he touches her and is invisible, and writes her notes without hands. It is possible that amorous spirits have known this for a long time, but Charles Vincent had made the discovery himself independently.

When enough knowledge is accumulated on any subject, the pattern will sometimes emerge suddenly, like a form in a picture revealed where before it was not seen. And when enough knowledge is accumulated on all subjects, is there not a chance that a pattern governing all subjects will emerge?

Charles Vincent was caught up in one last enthusiasm. On a long vigil, as he consulted source after source and sorted them in his mind, it seemed that the pattern was coming out clearly and simply, for all its amazing complexity of detail.

"I know everything that they know in the pit, and I know a secret that they do not know. I have not lost the race—I have won it. I can defeat them at the point where they believe themselves invulnerable. If controlled hereafter, we need at least not be controlled by them. It is all falling together now. I have found the final truth, and it is they who have lost the race. I hold the key. I will now be able to enjoy the advantage without paying the ultimate price of defeat and destruction, or of collaboration with them.

"Now I have only to implement my knowledge, to publish the fact, and one shadow at least will be lifted from mankind. I will do it at once. Well, nearly at once. It is almost dawn in the normal world. I will sit here a very little while and rest. Then I will go out and begin to make contact with the proper persons for the disposition of this thing. But first I will sit here a little while and rest."

And he died quietly in his chair as he sat there.

D R. MASON made an entry in his private journal: "Charles Vincent, a completely authenticated case of premature aging, one of the most clear-cut in all gerontology. This man was known to me for years, and I here aver that as of one year ago he was of normal appearance and physical state, and that his chronology is also correct, I having also known his father. I examined the subject during the period of his illness, and there is no question at all of his identity, which has also been established for the record by fingerprinting and other means. I aver that Charles Vincent at the age of thirty is dead of old age, having the appearance and organic condition of a man of ninety."

Then the doctor began to make another note: "As in two other cases of my own observation, the illness was accompanied by a certain delusion and series of dreams, so nearly identical in the three men as to be almost unbelievable. And for the record, and no doubt to the prejudice of my own reputation, I will set down the report of them here."

But when Dr. Mason had written that, he thought about it for a while.

"No, I will do no such thing," he said, and he struck out the last lines he had written. "It is best to let sleeping dragons lie."

And somewhere the faceless men with the smell of the pit on them smiled to themselves in quiet irony.

END

LIST OF CONTRIBUTORS

Editor
   Kevin Cheek

Proofreaders
   John Owen, Rich Persaud, Daniel Otto Jack Petersen, Noah
   Wareness

Publishing
   John Owen

Essays
   John Barach, Kevin Cheek, Elaine Cochrane, John Ellison,
   John Ellison, Andrew Ferguson, Martin Heavisides, Andrew
   Mass, Gregorio Montejo, John Owen, Rich Persaud, Daniel
   Otto Jack Petersen, Eric Walker

Poetry
   Kevin Cheek, David Cruces

Fiction
   Michael Bishop, R. A. Lafferty, Daniel Otto Jack Petersen, J
   Simon, Noah Wareness

Artwork
   Lissanne Lake, Daniel Otto Jack Petersen, Jack-Lewis
   Petersen, Lydia Petersen

Communication & Recruiting
   Kevin Cheek, John Owen, Rich Persaud, Daniel Otto Jack
   Petersen

Interview
   John Owen